THE FOOLPROOF AIR FRYER COOKBOOK

101 HEALTHY RESTAURANT-QUALITY MEALS AT HOME (WITH INSTRUCTIONS & ILLUSTRATIONS)

BY
LAURA BRYANS

healthy happy foodie

HEALTHY HAPPY FOODIE PRESS
SAN FRANCISCO, CA

COPYRIGHT © 2020 Healthy Happy Foodie Press (HHF Press)

First published 2020

All rights reserved. No part of this book may be reproduced in any form or by any electronic or mechanical means, including information storage and retrieval systems, without permission in writing from the publisher, except by reviewers, who may quote brief passages in a review.

Editor: HHF Press

Art Direction: HHF Press

Illustrations: HHF Press

All photographs in this book © HHF Press or © Depositphotos.com

healthy happy Foodie

Published in the United States of America by HHF Press
268 Bush St, #3042
San Francisco, CA 94104 USA
www.HHFPress.com

Disclaimer:

Although the publisher and author of this book are practically obsessed with modern cooking techniques, neither represent, nor are associated or affiliated with, any of the brands mentioned in this text.

All content herein represents the author's own experiences and opinions, and do not represent medical or health advice. The responsibility for the consequences of your actions, including your use or misuse of any suggestion or procedure described in this book lies not with the authors, publisher or distributors of this book. We recommend consulting with a licensed health professional before changing your diet or exercise. The author or the publisher does not assume any liability for the use of or inability to use any or all of the information contained in this book, nor does the author or publisher accept responsibility for any type of loss or damage that may be experienced by the user as the result of activities occurring from the use of any information in this book. Use the information responsibly and at your own risk.

The author reServings the right to make changes he or she deems required to future versions of the publication to maintain accuracy.

Reader Reviews

Thank you for this gorgeous book in air fryers! With the help of this book, I've become an expert at using my air fryer and I use it all the time! No more guilt...I feel very satisfied with how these recipes hit the "fried food" spot but without all of the baggage of regular fried foods. I especially loved the French Toast Sticks... and my kids love them even more...

Jay R.

I didn't think you could make so many desserts in an air fryer! Yesterday I made buttermilk banana blueberry bread...wow! The nutritional info is super helpful in deciding which recipe to make. My husband needs to watch his sodium intake so I'm able to choose recipes that are delicious but healthy too. Thanks! I recommend this book to anyone who has an air fryer!

Selena G.

The 10 minute quick start was really helpful, I didn't think I could make my first air fried food so quickly and easily! Now I feel very confident about making almost any recipe in this book, and I'm very eager to try some new ones. A-plus :)

Gemma B.

OK, Fried Chickpeas are an amazing snack! So are just about any other recipe I've made in my air fryer since getting this book. The recipe instructions are clear, and the book is really beautifully laid out with photos and good information. I especially like the collection of recipes, they are great for adults and kids alike.

Belina M.

We made crispy onion straws last night, just to try them out as a snack. They were better than onion rings! Thank you for such a well written and nice looking book. Everyone was excited to look through it, and we all pointed out some recipes to try. I'm keeping this book in the kitchen so it's handy.

Kimmy G.

Introduction

Who This Book Is For?

If you have just purchased, or already own, an air fryer then you need this book! Here's why:

Get the Most Out of Your Air Fryer Experience!

Illustrated instructions, a quick start guide and beyond-the-manual tips and tricks will teach you how to get the most out of your air fryer so that air frying becomes your family's favorite way to cook just about anything.

Get a Fast Start with "10 Minute Quick-Start"!

Our illustrated "10 Minute Quick-Start" chapter will walk you through your first complete meal in under 10 minutes, so you can quickly enjoy delicious meats, vegetables, breakfast, desserts, and much more instead of spending all of your time reading instruction manuals.

Clear, Illustrated Instructions!

Will make your air fryer experience so simple you can start cooking in minutes while avoiding beginner mistakes such as wrong settings, wrong timing, etc.

Go Beyond the Instruction Manual!

Our Pro tips will have you cooking like the pros in no time. Learn the science behind air frying cooking so that you can confidently make the best, most nutritious meals you've ever had.

Unbiased Recommendations, Workarounds, and Pro Tips!

To help you confidently make amazing meals that are perfectly tailored to your family, while avoiding common mistakes, wherever you go!

All the Recipes You'll Ever Need!

101 of the best air fryer recipes on the planet will allow you to make the classic breakfasts, lunches, and dinners you are already familiar with, as well as fun and exciting recipes which will give your family the variety they love.

Contents

ABOUT Air Frying 1

HOW TO USE an Air Fryer 5

10 minute Quick-Start 10-11

Pro Tips 13

Breakfast Dishes 21
French Toast Sticks 22
Ham & Egg Toast Cups 23
Hash Browns 25
Bacon Egg & Cheese Eggroll 26
Air Fryer Breakfast Potatoes 27
Blueberry Lemon Muffins 28
Cinnamon Rolls 30
Apple Fritter Rings 31
Cinnamon Sugar Muffins 33
Sausage Balls 34
All in One Breakfast Sandwich 35

Appetizers 37
Mac & Cheese Bites 38
Buffalo Cauliflower 39
Crispy Kale Chips 41
Air-Fried Green Tomatoes 42
Bacon Wrapped Shrimp 43
Crab Cakes 44
Cheddar Bacon Croquettes 46
Veggie Fritters 47
Avocado Fries 49
Stuffed Mushrooms 50
Cheddar Biscuits 51
Fried Artichoke Hearts 52
Fried Pickles 54
Crispy Eggplant Caprese Stacks 55
Crab Rangoon 56
Jalapeño Poppers 57

Poultry Dishes 59
Sweet & Spicy Firecracker Chicken 60
Fried Chicken Livers 61
Chicken Parmesan 63
Turkey with Maple Mustard Glaze 64
Buttermilk Fried Chicken 65
Chicken Fajita Roll Ups 66
Crispy Coconut Chicken 67
Tandoori Chicken 68
Homemade Chicken Nuggets 70
Buffalo Chicken Meatballs 71
Chicken Wontons 72
Chicken Kabobs 73

Beef, Lamb & Pork Dishes 75

- Cheese Burger Eggrolls 76
- Roasted Stuffed Peppers 77
- Country Fried Steak 78
- Chinese Beef Spare Ribs 79
- Air FryerBurgers 81
- Steak Roll Ups 82
- Coffee & Chili Rub Steak 83
- Marinated Beef Tips 84
- Crispy Fried Pork Cutlets 85
- Meatloaf 86
- Bacon Cheeseburger Bombs 88
- Bacon Wrapped Hot Dog 89
- Air Fryer Strip Steak 90
- Adobo Crusted Lamb Loin Chops 91
- Roast Beef 93
- Lamb Kofta Kabobs 94
- Tuscan Pork Chops 95
- Asian Pork Chops 96
- Simple FriedPork Chops 97

Seafood 99

- Fried Squid with Aioli 100
- Fried Scallops 101
- Easy Fried Cod Filets 103
- Shrimp & Mango Spring Rolls 104
- Potato Crusted Salmon 105
- Fried Fish Tacos 106
- Indian Fish Fingers 108
- Old Bay Crab Cakes 109
- Salmon Croquettes 111
- Quick Fried Catfish 112
- Oyster Sandwiches 113
- Japanese Style Fried Shrimp 114
- Shrimp Wontons 115

Vegetables & Side Dishes 117

- Roasted Corn 118
- Seasoned Potato Wedges 119
- Home Made Tater Tots 121
- Honey Roasted Carrots 122
- Onion Rings 123
- Garlic Parmesan Fries 124
- Baked Sweet Potato 125
- Roasted Brussels Sprouts 126
- Vermouth Roasted Mushrooms 128
- Lemony Green Beans 129
- Crispy Onion Straws 130
- Twice Baked Potato 131
- Zucchini Fries 133
- Crispy Roasted Broccoli 134
- Fried Chickpeas 135
- Skinny Carrot Fries 136
- Crispy Enoki & Onion Fritters 137
- Potato Chips 138
- California Fried Walnuts 140
- Fried Artichokes 141
- Fried Plantains 142
- Rosemary Sweet Potato Fries 143

Desserts 145

- Mini Chocolate Molten Lava Cakes 146
- Fried Banana S'mores 147
- Monkey Bread 149
- Blueberry Apple Crumble 150
- Apple Pie to Go 151
- Chocolate Chip Muffins 152
- Blackberry Hand Pies 154
- Buttermilk Banana Blueberry Bread 155

CHAPTER 1

About Air Frying

What is Air Frying?

We're all familiar with traditional fried foods. Chances are, some of your favorite foods are fried, but since you know they're not the healthiest foods you could be eating, they come with guilt attached. So, how can you have your (fried) cake and eat it too (without guilt)? Well, modern cooking technology has solved this problem by creating...drum roll... the Air Fryer. The miraculous modern air fryer is an easy to use, compact device that allows you to make all of your favorite fried foods, at home, but in a much healthier way. Now you can enjoy delicious French fries, fried chicken, and so much more without the guilt or negative impacts to your health attached to normally fried foods. By using only a small amount of oil and a revolutionary cooking system, you no longer have to compromise your health for flavor.

What Does an Air Fryer Do?

Air fryers fry foods without using so much oil by using a heating element on one end of the unit and a fan on the other. The fan circulates super-heated air around the food, cooking it from the outside in, and creating the same effect (called the Maillard reaction) that you achieve with traditionally fried foods. The difference is that instead of using a large amount of oil, air fryers use calorie-free air. Many recipes still call for a little oil, but it's only a fraction of what you'd use with most traditional frying methods, so the potential risk to your health from eating high amounts of trans fats is greatly reduced. Now you can feel free to start enjoying your favorite foods!

What Does an Air Fryer NOT Do?

While air frying is a perfect way to prepare your favorite fried foods while only using a small amount of oil, there are a few things it will not do. Certain fried foods that are batter- or liquid-based (like funnel cakes) require a full oil bath in order to cook externally and internally. While an air fryer is the perfect way to heat up any of your favorite fried foods, cooking battered foods will require a little extra preparation. Because batter tends to be runny, it may have trouble sticking to your food as it cooks in the air fryer. As a result, you will need to use recipes which are specifically designed for air fryers. Luckily this book contains a bunch of great air fryer friendly recipes for battered foods. Our 10 Minute Quick-Start will get you started cooking battered foods in minutes!

Who uses Air Fryers?

Because air fryers are able to rival the results of conventional deep fryers, they are great for anyone who wants the rich, satisfying flavor of traditional fried foods, but without the hassle, mess or health risks of conventional frying. Frying can be a messy proposition, especially if you are cooking at home without a powerful range hood. As a result, your kitchen can become coated in sticky oil which can be difficult to clean. Home chefs who don't want to deal with all of that mess will find that air fryers are the perfect way to make your favorite foods without dealing with so much oil. Air fryers are also great for those who want a healthier way to make fried foods. Because they use only a small amount of oil, far less oil is absorbed by your food, which means you can cook foods that are healthier while still being flavorful.

The History of Air Frying

Air frying is actually a very new cooking concept and wasn't introduced to the market until 2010. Prior to this, the only way to fry was to submerge food in a vat of cooking oil. This new technology, however, finally allowed home cooks to get the same results that restaurants achieve, but without the use of cumbersome deep fryers and huge quantities of oil. The result is a way to get perfectly crispy fried foods without the mess of deep frying, and using only a tiny amount of oil. Not only is air frying easier, it's also much more healthy!

Health Benefits

The health benefits of air frying are perhaps the best reason to consider this cooking method. The main problem with traditional deep frying isn't the food you are cooking, but rather the oil used in the cooking process. Traditional deep frying requires you to fully submerge your food in oil, and as a result, your food absorbs a lot of that oil. The problem is that oil contains a lot of calories, fat, and often cholesterol. Because these oils mix with the carbohydrates in your food, you end up with one of the unhealthiest combinations possible. Air fryers, on the other hand, only use a tiny amount of oil. Because they are able to use circulating hot air to cook your food, the amount of oil can be greatly reduced, which means you are not eating nearly as much fat. This leads to lighter foods which are not only better for you, they actually taste lighter and are more flavorful.

Aside from the calorie count, the biggest negative factor of oil frying is that it is downright dangerous. How many times have you thrown something into oil and then ran the other direction to avoid the hot oil splatter? It's not only unpleasant, it's unsafe.

If there is one concern more important than burning your skin it may be burning your whole house down. The lack of oil frying means there is no oil to start a kitchen fire which could eventually lead to a house fire.

Cautions

Obviously, your air fryer is much safer than traditional deep frying because it uses far less oil in order to cook. However, it does still use a small amount of oil which will be very hot after cooking. In order to serve the freshest, crispiest fried foods, you will want to serve your food immediately following cooking. To avoid burns, always make sure to use cooking tongs to remove food from the basket. Also, make sure the fryer has completed its cooking program and has turned itself off before you remove the basket from the fryer. Because the small amount of oil is being heated by super-hot circulated air, you can end up burning yourself if you try to open the fryer before it has finished cooking.

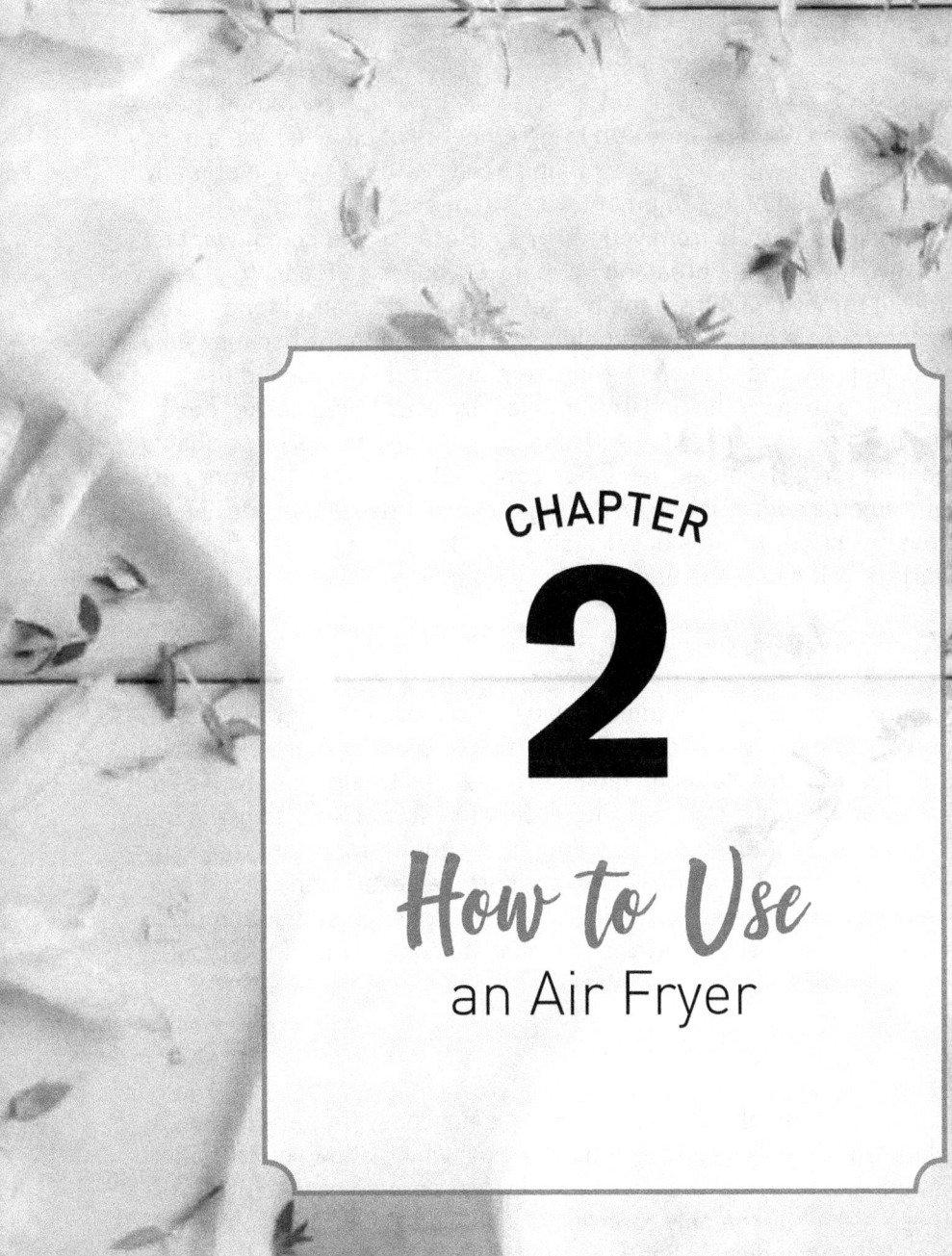

CHAPTER 2

How to Use an Air Fryer

Equipment you will need

One of the great things about air fryers is how self-contained they are. Instead of using pots and large amounts of oil, you have a handy machine that will handle your frying needs without the use of many pieces of additional equipment. You will need a few things to help get the best results from your air fryer. Because you do not want to disturb the delicate breading on many of your fried foods, the best way to remove food from the basket is by using a pair of tongs. We recommend a set of long handled silicon tipped tongs because they will keep your hands safely away from any heat source, and the silicon coating on the ends will make sure your frying basket does not become damaged. You will also want to purchase a good quality cooling rack. Because fried foods come out best when they are not placed on a solid surface, a cooling rack will ensure that your food remains crispy on all sides. Placing your food on a plate or flat surface will cause the underside of your food to become soggy.

Setting Up and Using your Air Fryer

Before you even put anything in your fryer there are a few things you are going to want to do. First of all, you want to make sure that your fryer is on a flat and stable surface, even though it only uses a small amount of oil, it can still get very hot so you want to make sure it is perfectly stable before cooking. It is equally important that you place your fryer on a burn-resistant surface because the frying can become hot. Make sure that the fryer is plugged in and attach the basket to the device. Now you are ready to cook some of the most delicious, healthy food you have ever had.

Learning the Controls

The great thing about most air fryers is how easy they are to use. Most feature only several simple controls which allow you to control timing and temperature. Because air fryers are so easy to use, these are really the only controls you will need. Typically, you will also find two indicator lights on the front or top of your air fryer. These lights indicate that the fryer is on, and that is has come to the proper cooking temperature. Only place your food in the fryer basket, and always make sure the basket is properly installed before commencing the cooking process.

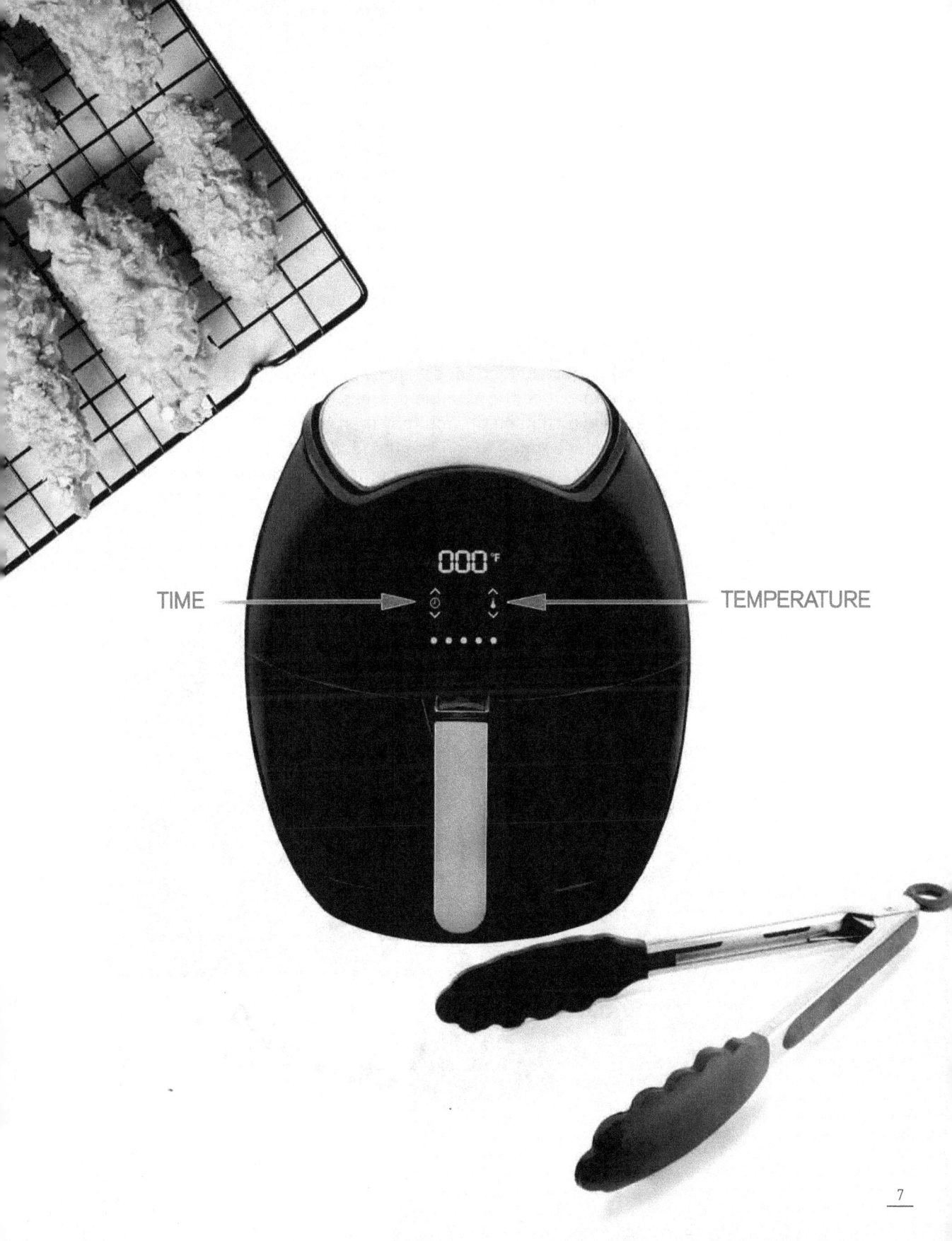

The Cooking Process

The great thing about cooking with an air fryer is that you don't need to do very much during the cooking process. Once you have set the temperature and time knobs, the fryer will quickly begin heating using a heating element and a circulating fan. The process, which will evenly distribute the heat around the food, is quite similar to convection cooking, however, the unique design of the interior of the fryer is perfectly suited to allow the heat to circulate around the food evenly and quickly. Because frying relies on a balance between cooking the interior of the food and making sure the outside does not burn, your air fryer is specifically designed to take all of the guesswork out of cooking tender, juicy food with a perfectly golden brown exterior. Once the cooking process has finished, the fryer will automatically turn itself off. You may then remove the basket from the fryer and use tongs to remove the food from the basket. Always make sure to give your food a few moments to cool before eating as the hot oil on the exterior of the food will be extremely hot.

Troubleshooting

PROBLEM	SOLUTION
White smoke is coming out of my air fryer!	Chances are, this is steam. Most likely, the cause is too much moisture. It is recommended that your food has been dried so there is no water on the surface. If you find that steam is coming from your air fryer, turn it off, allow it to cool, and then make sure to pat dry your food.
Black smoke is coming out of my air fryer!	Most likely this is caused by food being too fatty. In the future, you can attempt to trim excess fat from your food, or you can place a small amount of water in the bottom of the frying basket to absorb dripping grease. This may help to keep the smoke from escaping the fryer.
Blue smoke is coming out of my air fryer!	While this problem is rare, it may mean you have an electrical problem with your air fryer. If you experience blue smoke, immediately turn off your fryer and consult with the manufacturer.
There is a lingering food smell after I use my air fryer.	Most likely, this happens because you have not properly cleaned your air fryer after using it. Small food particles can go unnoticed. They can end up getting cooked again when you use your fryer again. To combat this, make sure that you remove all trays and baskets from your fryer and thoroughly clean everything each time you cook.
I can't get a nice, crispy exterior on my food.	While many air fryer manuals claim that you do not need to use oil when air frying, this is not always the case. If you find that your food is not crispy, try applying a small amount of oil to your food with either a brush or a spray can.
Some of my food is overcooked and some of it is undercooked.	If you are getting uneven results, it's usually because you are overloading the frying basket. Try cooking in batches and make sure the food has enough room to cook evenly.

10 Minute Quick-Start

We're going to start with a classic breakfast staple the whole family will love which is easy to make and even more delicious when cooked in your air fryer. We're talking, of course, about French toast. These fun French toast sticks will come out of your air fryer soft in the middle and perfectly crispy on the outside.

1 Collect These Ingredients:

- 4 slices thick cut white or brioche bread
- 2 eggs
- 1/4 cup whole milk
- 1/4 cup brown sugar
- 1 teaspoon cinnamon
- Nutmeg to taste
- Fresh berries, honey or jam for serving

2 Collect These Tools:

- Your air Fryer
- Chef's knife
- Large bowl
- Whisk

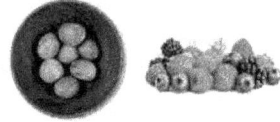

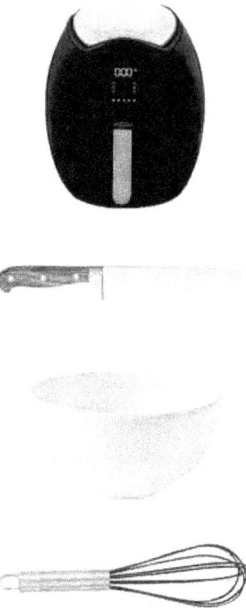

The goal of 10 minute Quick-Start is to walk you through making your first meal so you "learn by doing" in under 10 minutes. Once you've had a chance to get familiar with how your air fryer works, you can begin experimenting with all different types of foods!

 Follow These **Steps:**

1. Cut each slice of bread vertically into 4 equal strips.
2. Beat the eggs in a large bowl, then mix remaining ingredients together in the same bowl.
3. Dip each bread strip into the bowl allowing all excess batter to drip off.
4. Preheat the air fryer to 360°F and place each strip in the basket.
5. Cook for 10 minutes, flipping them over at the halfway point. Serve with fresh berries, honey or sweet jam.

Congratulations!

You've just made your first breakfast and learned the basics of how to use your air fryer. Time to celebrate with the whole family!

# CHAPTER 3

Pro Tips

Make Sure Your Food is Dry Before Frying

One of the biggest complaints about the actual process of frying foods the traditional way is the smoke and smell that come along with it. This doesn't happen with an air fryer as long as you make sure that your food is not wet when you put it in the air fryer. Foods don't have to be completely dry, after all, you will still need to use a little oil here and there, but they should not be dripping wet. If your food is too wet, you will notice a thick white smoke with an odor coming from your machine. To avoid this issue, pat down your food with a dry paper towel before placing it in the basket. If there is a large amount of smoke coming from your fryer, don't worry, just stop your timer, dry the food, and restart the timer. This should stop the smoke and prevent any further issues. If the problem continues, you may have to wait it out a few minutes. If it continues to smoke, use your judgement to decide whether to pat dry and try again or to turn off the air fryer and stop cooking the smoking food.

Do Not Overfill the Air Fryer Basket

While you may be tempted to cook all of your food at once, this can cause serious problems with an air fryer. Most commonly, you will end up with unevenly-cooked food and no one wants that. You may also find that your air fryer emits smoke when the basket is too full, or that the machine overheats and simply stops working. To avoid this, always follow the guidelines set out for your specific air fryer for how much food to cook in a single batch. Cooking in batches will ensure that your results are always perfectly even and delicious.

To keep your cooked food warm as you cook in batches, simply set your oven to warm or around 200F and your food will stay warm and crispy until you are ready to serve.

Use a Cooling Rack

Even though you are frying with a small amount of oil, you are still frying food, which means that the outside of your food is going to be crispy and you want to keep it that way. When you place fried foods on a flat surface residual heat builds up underneath the food and creates steam which will make your foods soggy. By placing fried foods on a cooling rack, it allows that heat to escape which will keep your food crispier longer. This is a perfect way to store fried foods if you are cooking multiple servings for supper or making a large batch that will be served in 4 hours or less.

How to Store Fried Food

If you need to store your food in a refrigerator it's best to let them fully cool before storing them. Use the cooling rack method to let all of the excess heat evaporate and make sure that the food is completely cool (sometimes up to 2 hours) before placing your food in plastic storage containers. You can also pierce small holes in the top of the storage containers to allow condensation to release. Food stored in storage containers can last up to a week or more. When you are ready to eat your stored food, you can always pop it back in the air fryer for a few minutes to heat up. It may not be quite as fresh as when it was first fried, but it should maintain crispness and flavor. Baked goods which have been cooked in your air fryer are best stored in paper bags or plastic wrap. This will allow them to stay fresher, longer.

Season After Frying

Once you've successfully fried food in your air fryer there is an important last step before you enjoy what you've created: seasoning. Many methods of cooking benefit from seasoning prior to cooking because it adds flavor to the food as it cooks. This is also true of fried foods, however, there is an important step that professional chefs know that you should know as well. When you first remove your food from the fryer it will still have a thin layer of liquid oil. This creates the perfect opportunity to add flavor, but you need to act quickly. As soon as you remove food from the fryer and place it on the cooling rack, immediately sprinkle your food with salt. The liquid oil will quickly dry, leaving your food with a nice, crispy exterior, but if you've added salt to that liquid oil, it will be locked into the food as the oil dries. This way, every bite is guaranteed to be perfectly seasoned.

Flavor Building

The best way to start building flavors is with a general seasoning with salt and black pepper. You can also experiment with these herbs and spices to build fun, new flavors with different proteins.

BEEF	SALMON	PORK	CHICKEN	VEGETABLES
Shallots	Lemon Pepper	Mustard	Rosemary	Olive Oil
Garlic	Citrus	Thyme	Garlic	Thyme
Thyme	Paprika	White Wine	White Wine	Mint
Cumin	Dill	Apple Cider	Thyme	Onion Powder
Rosemary	Basil	Rosemary	Soy Sauce	
Red Wine	Olive Oil		Lemon Pepper	
			Olive Oil	

Wine and Beer Pairing

Try these varieties with your favorite meats and fish.

NEW YORK OR RIBEYE STEAKS

Wine	Beer
Cabernet Sauvignon	IPA
Malbec	Brown Ale
Shiraz	Stout

SALMON

Wine	Beer
Sauvignon Blanc	Pilsner
Pinot Grigio	Lager
Riesling	IPA

PORK

Wine	Beer
Chardonnay	Brown Ale
Pinot Noir	IPA
	Stout

WHITE FISHES

Wine	Beer
Sauvignon Blanc	Light Ale
Chardonnay	Pilsner
	Hefeweissen

CHICKEN

Wine	Beer
Sauvignon Blanc	Pilsner
Merlot	Lager
Pinot Noir	Light Ale

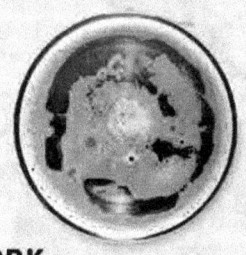

Time and Temperatures

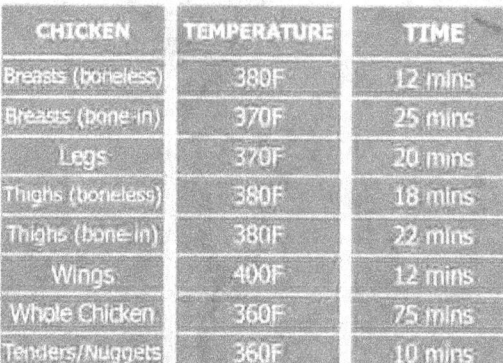

VEGETABLES	TEMPERATURE	TIME
Asparagus	400F	5 mins
Beets	400F	40 mins
Broccoli	400F	6 mins
Brussels Sprouts	380F	15 mins
Carrots	380F	15 mins
Cauliflower	400F	12 mins
Corn (on cob)	390F	6 mins
Eggplant	400F	15 mins
Green Beans	400F	5 mins
Kale	250F	12 mins
Mushrooms	400F	5 mins
Onions	400F	10 mins
Peppers	400F	15 mins
Potatoes (chunks)	400F	15 mins
Potatoes (whole)	400F	40 mins
Squash	400F	12 mins
Sweet Potato	380F	30 mins
Tomatoes	400F	4 mins
Zucchini	400F	12 mins

CHICKEN	TEMPERATURE	TIME
Breasts (boneless)	380F	12 mins
Breasts (bone-in)	370F	25 mins
Legs	370F	20 mins
Thighs (boneless)	380F	18 mins
Thighs (bone-in)	380F	22 mins
Wings	400F	12 mins
Whole Chicken	360F	75 mins
Tenders/Nuggets	360F	10 mins

BEEF	TEMPERATURE	TIME
Burger	370F	18 mins
Filet Mignon	400F	18 mins
Flank Steak	400F	12 mins
Meatballs	380F	7 mins
Ribeye Steak	400F	10 - 15 mins
Sirloin Steak	400F	9 - 14 mins

PORK	TEMPERATURE	TIME
Loin	360F	55 mins
Chops	400F	12 mins
Tenderloin	370F	15 mins
Bacon	400F	5 mins
Sausages	380F	15 mins

FROZEN FOOD	TEMPERATURE	TIME
Onion Rings	400F	8 mins
French Fries (thin)	400F	14 mins
French Fries (thick)	400F	18 mins
Mozzarella Sticks	400F	8 mins
Pot Stickers	400F	8 mins
Fish Sticks	400F	10 mins
Chicken Nuggets	400F	10 mins
Breaded Shrimp	400F	9 mins

SEAFOOD	TEMPERATURE	TIME
Calamari	400F	4 mins
Fish Filet	400F	10 mins
Salmon	380F	12 mins
Swordfish	400F	10 mins
Scallops	400F	5 mins
Shrimp	400F	5 mins

Choosing Your Oil

For most foods, a little oil will be necessary to get the results you want. But don't worry, a little oil goes a long way. But what kind of oil should you use to get the best results? When choosing your oil, there are two things to consider. First: what kind of flavor would you like? And second: at what temperature will you be cooking? If you want a very neutral tasting oil, try using grapeseed or canola oil. These oils can also be used at higher temperatures without smoking. If you are cooking at a lower temperature and you want to add earthy flavor to your food, olive oil will provide a lot of flavor and it's a healthy oil as well. If you want truly decadent flavor and you're not trying to make a healthy meal, try peanut oil. It's not as good for you as olive oil, but it's what many restaurants use to make delicious fries.

CHAPTER 4

Breakfast

French Toast Sticks

This is a family favorite because it's easy to make and the kids can't get enough of the great taste.

Servings: 2
Prep Time: 5 minutes
Cook Time: 10 minutes

4 slices whole meal bread
2 eggs
1/4 cup whole milk
1/4 cup brown sugar
1 teaspoon cinnamon
Nutmeg to taste
Fresh berries, honey or jam for serving

1. Cut each slice of bread vertically into 4 equal strips.
2. Beat the eggs in a large bowl, then mix remaining ingredients together in the same bowl.
3. Dip each bread strip into the bowl allowing all excess batter to drip off.
4. Preheat the air fryer to 360°F and place each strip in the basket.
5. Cook for 10 minutes, flipping them over at the halfway point. Serve with fresh berries, honey or sweet jam.

Nutrition

Calories: 283, Sodium: 79 mg, Dietary Fiber: 0.6 g, Fat: 6.4 g, Carbs: 45.1 g, Protein: 10.7 g.

Ham & Egg Toast Cups

This is a great little breakfast treat that allows you to create a full morning meal inside of your air fryer.

Servings: 2
Prep Time: 10 minutes
Cook Time: 15 minutes

2 ramekins
2 eggs
4 slices of bread
1 slice of ham
Melted butter
Salt and pepper, to taste

1. Brush the inside of the ramekins with melted butter.
2. Toast bread and flatten it with a rolling pin.
3. Press 1 piece of toast into the bottom of each ramekin to create a bread bowl.
4. Press another piece of toast onto the first one to create a double layer.
5. Cut the ham into 4 slices, then line the inside of the toast cups with 2 strips of ham each.
6. Crack an egg into the center of each cup and season with salt and pepper.
7. Cook in the air fryer for 15 minutes at 320°F. If you like your eggs less runny, you may want to add a few minutes to the cook time.

Nutrition
Calories: 202, Sodium: 488 mg, Dietary Fiber: 1.6 g, Fat: 10.2 g, Carbs: 16 g, Protein: 9.2 g.

Hash Browns

Hash browns are a breakfast staple and when you use your air fryer, you are guaranteed to get the crispiest hash browns every time.

Servings: 8
Prep Time: 35 minutes
Cook Time: 15 minutes

4 russet potatoes
2 tablespoons corn flour
1 teaspoon garlic powder
1 teaspoon onion powder
2 teaspoons olive oil, separated
Salt and pepper, to taste

1. Peel and shred your potatoes.
2. Soak potatoes in water, then drain and repeat to remove excess starch.
3. Heat 1 teaspoon olive oil in a pan and sauté the potatoes for a few minutes.
4. Mix the potatoes and all the dry ingredients until well mixed.
5. Flatten them out over a plate and refrigerate for 20 minutes.
6. Preheat the air fryer to 360°F.
7. Cut your hash browns into squares and place them in the basket brushing them with a little oil.
8. Cook for 15 minutes, flipping halfway through.

Nutrition
Calories: 92, Sodium: 7 mg, Dietary Fiber: 2.7 g, Fat: 1.4 g, Carbs: 18.6 g, Protein: 2 g.

Bacon Egg & Cheese Eggroll

I don't know what's better about this recipe: how great it tastes or the fact that these can be taken on the go.

Servings: 5
Prep Time: 15 minutes
Cook Time: 10 minutes

4 eggs
4 slices bacon
1/2 cup shredded cheddar cheese
5 egg roll wrappers

1. In a large skillet, cook the bacon until crisp and set aside.
2. Drain the bacon fat but leave a little left behind in the skillet.
3. Using the bacon fat, scramble your eggs.
4. Roll out your eggroll wrappers.
5. In a separate bowl, crumble the bacon into tiny pieces, then mix in the eggs and the cheese.
6. Scoop in equal amounts of the mixture to the center of each wrapper.
7. Pull the bottom left corner of the wrapper over the mixture, then fold each side in.
8. Wet the remaining edge and roll the eggroll shut.
9. Preheat your air fryer at 360°F and cook for 10 minutes, flipping eggrolls halfway through.

Nutrition

Calories: 271, Sodium: 654 mg, Dietary Fiber: 0.6 g, Fat: 14.1 g, Carbs: 19.2 g, Protein: 16 g.

Air Fryer Breakfast Potatoes

This is a fantastic recipe because it can be used as a breakfast side or mixed in with some eggs and sausage to create a healthy breakfast bowl.

Servings: 4
Prep Time: 10 minutes
Cook Time: 25 minutes

2 russet potatoes
1 red bell pepper
1 white onion
Cooking spray
Salt and pepper, to taste.

1. Cut the potatoes into small 1 inch cubes.
2. Put them in the basket, spray with cooking spray and sprinkle with a little salt and pepper.
3. Cook the potatoes at 390°F for 10 minutes, shaking once at the halfway point.
4. While waiting for the potatoes to cook, dice up the peppers and onions into small cubes.
5. Mix in the onions and peppers with the potatoes. Season it with salt and pepper.
6. Using the air fryer, cook at 390°F for another 15 minutes. Shake a few times and make sure that the potatoes aren't overcooked.

Nutrition
Calories: 94, Sodium: 8 mg, Dietary Fiber: 3.6 g, Fat: 0.2 g, Carbs: 21.6 g, Protein: 2.4 g.

Blueberry Lemon Muffins

People don't realize how versatile an air fryer can be until they try out an amazing baked recipe like this one. Serve with a hot cup of coffee!

Servings: 6
Prep Time: 10 minutes
Cook Time: 10 minutes

2-1/2 cups self-rising flour
1/2 cup sugar
1/2 cup cream
1/4 cup olive oil
2 eggs
1 cup blueberries
2 tablespoons lemon juice
1 teaspoon vanilla

1. Mix flour and sugar together in a small bowl.
2. In a large bowl combine cream, oil, and eggs until well blended; then add lemon juice and vanilla, mixing well.
3. Add the flour mix to the wet ingredients and mix well.
4. Put cupcake holders in the fryer basket and fill each with batter.
5. Using the air fryer, cook at 320°F for 10 minutes.

Nutrition
Calories: 375, Sodium: 79 mg, Dietary Fiber: 2 g, Fat: 11.6 g, Carbs: 60.8 g, Protein: 7.6 g.

Cinnamon Rolls

Yes, your air fryer can even make delicious cinnamon rolls without having to fire up your oven. Delicious served with coffee or chai.

Servings: 8
Prep Time: 20 minutes
Cook Time: 10 minutes

Rolls:

- 1 lb. frozen bread dough
- 1/4 cup melted butter
- 3/4 cup brown sugar
- 1-1/2 tablespoons ground cinnamon

Cream Cheese Glaze:

- 4 ounces cream cheese
- 2 tablespoons butter
- 1-1/4 cups powdered sugar
- 1/2 teaspoon vanilla

1. Allow dough to thaw before use.
2. Roll the dough into a 13 x 11-inch rectangle with the wider part facing you.
3. Mix the brown sugar and cinnamon together.
4. Melt the butter for the rolls and brush it evenly over the dough.
5. Sprinkle the brown sugar mix evenly over the dough.
6. Roll the dough into a tight tube starting at your end and rolling away from you.
7. Cut the tube into 8 pieces and lay them flat on a clean surface with a kitchen towel over them.
8. Allow the dough to rise for 2 hours.
9. Pull out your cream cheese and butter for the glaze to let it soften.
10. Preheat your air fryer to 350°F.
11. Once the rolls have risen, bake them in the air fryer for 10 minutes, flipping them halfway through.
12. While the rolls bake, mix together all of the ingredients for the cream cheese glaze.
13. Allow the cooked rolls to cool for 2 minutes, then top with the glaze.

Nutrition

Calories: 508, Sodium: 587 mg, Dietary Fiber: 2.5 g, Fat: 13.7 g, Carbs: 87.1 g, Protein: 11.2 g.

Apple Fritter Rings

Not only are these apple fritter rings delectable, but they are a fun shape that pleases the whole family.

Servings: 6
Prep Time: 20 minutes
Cook Time: 10 minutes

2 cups all-purpose flour
1/2 teaspoon baking powder
1/4 teaspoon ground nutmeg
1 teaspoon cinnamon
1/4 cup sugar
1/4 teaspoon salt
2 eggs
1-1/4 cups buttermilk
6 red apples
Powdered sugar, for finishing

1. Peel and core the apples, then cut each one into 6 rings.
2. Combine all of your dry ingredients in a bowl and mix well.
3. Add the eggs and buttermilk into the dry ingredients bowl and mix well.
4. Dip the apple rings in the batter and let any excess batter drip off.
5. Transfer rings to a sheet of parchment paper.
6. Lay about 6 rings (depending on size) in your basket. Cook at 320°F using the air fryer for 10 minutes, flipping at the halfway point. Serve with a sprinkle of powdered sugar!

Nutrition
Calories: 342, Sodium: 174 mg, Dietary Fiber: 6.8 g, Fat: 2.8 g, Carbs: 74 g, Protein: 8.5 g.

Cinnamon Sugar Muffins

Is it a donut? Is it a muffin? No one will care once one of these bad boys melts in their mouth.

Servings: 6
Prep Time: 20 minutes
Cook Time: 12 minutes

1-3/4 cups all-purpose flour
1-1/2 teaspoons baking powder
1/3 cup oil
1/2 teaspoon salt
1/2 teaspoon nutmeg
1/2 teaspoon cinnamon
1/2 teaspoon vanilla extract
3/4 cup sugar
1 egg
3/4 cup milk
Mini cupcake liners

1. Mix together flour, nutmeg, cinnamon, baking powder, and salt in a medium bowl.
2. In a large bowl combine oil, sugar, egg, milk, and vanilla.
3. Pour the dry ingredients into the larger bowl and fold over until combined, but not completely smooth.
4. Pour the mixture into your cupcake liners and transfer them to the basket.
5. Cook using the air fryer at 350°F for 12 minutes. Check a few times to make sure they are not baking too fast.

Nutrition

Calories: 286, Sodium: 219 mg, Dietary Fiber: 0.6 g, Fat: 13.7 g, Carbs: 39 g, Protein: 3.6 g.

Sausage Balls

This is a super versatile recipe that can be used for a breakfast on the go or a game day appetizer. These sausage balls are so savory they are hard not to love.

Servings: 10
Prep Time: 10 minutes
Cook Time: 20 minutes

1 lb. breakfast sausage
1 egg
1 cup bread crumbs
1 cup sharp cheddar cheese
2 teaspoons baking powder
1/2 teaspoon salt

1. Combine all ingredients in a large mixing bowl and mix well. Considering the consistency of these ingredients, you may want to use an electric mixer to save your shoulders.
2. Preheat your air fryer at 350°F.
3. Spoon out small scoops and roll them into balls and place them in your basket giving them room to breathe. This recipe makes about 30 balls, so you will probably have to do at least 2 batches.
4. Cook at 350°F for 20 minutes. Toss at the 10 and 15-minute mark.

Nutrition

Calories: 262, Sodium: 533 mg, Dietary Fiber: 1.2 g, Fat: 21.8 g, Carbs: 2.7 g, Protein: 14.2 g.

All in One
Breakfast Sandwich

This is a super simple recipe that is quick to make, on the healthy side, and can be taken on the go.

Servings: 1
Prep Time: 1 minute
Cook Time: 7 minutes

1 ramekin
1 egg
1 English muffin
2 pieces bacon
1 slice cheddar cheese
Salt and pepper, to taste

1. Break egg in the ramekin and add salt and pepper.
2. Preheat the air fryer to 390°F.
3. Place all the ingredients (except for the cheese) in the air fryer basket and cook for 6 minutes.
4. Assemble the sandwich in the following order: bottom of the muffin, the egg, the cheese, the bacon, and the top of the muffin. Serve hot!

Nutrition
Calories: 476, Sodium: 1038 mg, Dietary Fiber: 3 g, Fat: 26.6 g, Carbs: 32.2 g, Protein: 24.6 g.

CHAPTER 5

Appetizers

Mac & Cheese Bites

This recipe is ambitious, but attainable and the extra time it takes is well worth the results.

Servings: 4
Prep Time: 1 hour
Cook Time: 10 minutes

3 pieces bacon
3 cloves garlic
1/2 can beer
3/4 cups milk
2 cups elbow macaroni noodles
1-1/2 cups shredded cheddar cheese
1/4 cup grated parmesan cheese
3 eggs
1/2 cup flour
1/2 cup breadcrumbs
Salt & pepper, to taste

1. Cook the macaroni in a pot of boiling, salted water to al dente.
2. Meanwhile, dice your bacon and chop your garlic into fine pieces.
3. Cook the bacon until it begins to crisp, then add garlic and sauté for another minute.
4. Slowly mix in 3 tablespoons of flour until the mixture begins to turn into a paste.
5. Slowly add the milk and beer, making sure to stir continuously for about 5 minutes or until the sauce starts to take on a thicker consistency.
6. Add salt, pepper, and cheeses and mix until the cheese is completely melted.
7. Drain the macaroni. Place the macaroni in a bowl and mix in the cheese sauce until the macaroni is evenly coated throughout.
8. Place the mixture in the fridge for 45 minutes so it can set.
9. Beat the egg, place the breadcrumbs on a plate, and put the rest of the flour in a bowl or plate.
10. When the macaroni is set, remove it from the fridge. Take small handfuls and roll them into a ball.
11. Roll them in flour, dip them in egg, and then roll them in breadcrumbs until evenly coated.
12. Place them on the bottom of your basket making sure to give each ball room around it.
13. Cook in the air fryer at 360°F for 10 minutes.

Nutrition

Calories: 483, Sodium: 617 mg, Dietary Fiber: 1.7 g, Fat: 23.5 g, Carbs: 38 g, Protein: 26.6 g.

Buffalo Cauliflower

It turns out that it is possible to enjoy the delicious crunch and flavor of buffalo wings with a fraction of the calories.

Servings: 4
Prep Time: 10 minutes
Cook Time: 15 minutes

1 head cauliflower
1 cup panko breadcrumbs
1/4 cup butter
1/4 cup wing sauce

1. Combine butter and wing sauce in a bowl and microwave in 30-second increments until butter is completely melted. Mix well after each 30-second interval.
2. Cut cauliflower head into bite-sized florets.
3. Combine cauliflower and wing sauce in a bowl with a lid and toss until the cauliflower is completely coated.
4. Roll the cauliflower in breadcrumbs.
5. Cook using your air fryer for 350°F for 15 minutes, shaking the ingredient 2 times during the cooking process.

Nutrition

Calories: 147, Sodium: 219 mg, Dietary Fiber: 1.9 g, Fat: 12.1 g, Carbs: 8.7 g, Protein: 2.4 g.

Crispy Kale Chips

This simple recipe is one of the most perfect things you can cook in your air fryer. It is versatile, healthy, and has the perfect flavor and texture.

Servings: 1
Prep Time: 3 minutes
Cook Time: 3 minutes

1 head kale
1 tablespoon olive oil
Salt and pepper, to taste

1. Remove stem from kale and tear leaves into 1 - 2 inch "chips."
2. Place the chips into a sealable bowl and add oil, salt, and pepper.
3. Preheat your air fryer to 390°F.
4. Toss the ingredients until the chips are coated in oil.
5. Place in the air fryer and cook for 3 minutes, tossing halfway through.

Nutrition

Calories: 162, Sodium: 37 mg, Dietary Fiber: 1.3 g, Fat: 14 g, Carbs: 8.9 g, Protein: 2.5 g.

Air-Fried Green Tomatoes

It's hard to find a good fried green tomato, but now the search is over because you can make air-fried green tomatoes yourself at home with this recipe.

Servings: 6
Prep Time: 15 minutes
Cook Time: 20 minutes

- 4 green tomatoes
- 2 eggs
- 2 tablespoons milk
- 1 cup all-purpose flour
- 2 teaspoons garlic powder, separated
- 2 teaspoons paprika, separated
- 1/2 cup cornmeal
- 1/2 cup panko breadcrumbs

1. Wash and pat dry the tomatoes.
2. Cut them into 1/4-inch-thick circles and season with salt and pepper.
3. Beat the eggs in a bowl.
4. Combine flour, salt, pepper, 1 teaspoon garlic powder, and 1 teaspoon paprika.
5. In another bowl, combine cornmeal, breadcrumbs, garlic powder, and paprika.
6. Preheat your air fryer to 360°F.
7. Coat each tomato slice in flour, egg, then breadcrumbs.
8. Add a few at a time to your fryer and cook for 20 minutes, flipping halfway through.

Nutrition

Calories: 164, Sodium: 39 mg, Dietary Fiber: 2.7 g, Fat: 2.5 g, Carbs: 30 g, Protein: 6.3 g.

Bacon Wrapped Shrimp

This bite-sized appetizer is about as easy to make as you can get, but it will still disappear off a plate in seconds.

Servings: 4
Prep Time: 30 minutes
Cook Time: 7 minutes

1 lb. tiger shrimp
1 lb. bacon

1. Allow bacon to warm to room temperature.
2. While bacon warms, peel and devein shrimp.
3. Wrap each shrimp with bacon starting at the head and working your way down to the tail.
4. Refrigerate wrapped shrimp for 20 minutes.
5. Preheat your air fryer to 390°F.
6. Cook shrimp for 7 minutes, tossing once to ensure even cooking.
7. Place the shrimp on a paper towel to allow some of the bacon grease to drain before serving.

Nutrition
Calories: 726, Sodium: 2874 mg, Dietary Fiber: 0 g, Fat: 48.6 g, Carbs: 1.6 g, Protein: 65.7 g.

Crab Cakes

Crab cakes are not as hard to make as one might think and having the air fryer makes it even easier. This delicious recipe will make guests think that you are a genius in the kitchen.

Servings: 8
Prep Time: 15 minutes
Cook Time: 10 minutes

1 lb. crab meat
1 cup breadcrumbs or crushed butter crackers
1 egg
1 yellow onion
3 stalks spring onions
1 tablespoon mayonnaise
1 tablespoon corn flour
1/2 teaspoon garlic powder
1/2 teaspoon salt
Black pepper, to taste
1 pot of water

1. Chop your onions into fine pieces.
2. Boil the water and dunk the crabmeat in the boiling water for a few seconds.
3. Remove the crabmeat and pat it dry with paper towels.
4. Combine all of the ingredients in a large bowl and mix well, breaking up any large pieces of crabmeat.
5. Shape into patties and place in your air fryer basket. Cook for 5 minutes at 390°F.

Nutrition

Calories: 130, Sodium: 623 mg, Dietary Fiber: 1.1 g, Fat: 3 g, Carbs: 13.7 g, Protein: 9.9 g.

Cheddar Bacon Croquettes

These melt in your mouth croquettes are so delicious, your family is going to want them every night of the week.

Servings: 6
Prep Time: 35 minutes
Cook Time: 10 minutes

1 lb. sharp cheddar
1 lb. bacon
4 tablespoons olive oil
1 cup all-purpose flour
2 eggs
1 cup seasoned breadcrumbs

1. Cut the cheddar cheese block into six equal-sized pieces, about 1 by 1-3/4 inches.
2. Wrap bacon around each cheddar slice until the cheese is fully enclosed by bacon; trim off any extra.
3. Place the bacon and cheese in the freezer for about 5 minutes.
4. Meanwhile, mix together breadcrumbs and oil. Beat the eggs in a separate bowl and spread your flour in a shallow dish.
5. Preheat your air fryer to 390°F.
6. Remove the cheese from the freezer and roll it in flour, dip it in egg, then toss it in the breadcrumb mix.
7. Cook in the air fryer basket for 8 minutes and serve hot.

Nutrition

Calories: 743, Sodium: 965 mg, Dietary Fiber: 0.7 g, Fat: 59.6 g, Carbs: 22.3 g, Protein: 28.7 g.

Veggie Fritters

Being a vegetarian doesn't mean you have to eat like a rabbit all the time. This quick and easy recipe is so delicious that people won't even notice it's healthy!

Servings: 4
Prep Time: 20 minutes
Cook Time: 10 minutes

2 cups shredded zucchini
2 cups shredded carrots
2 cloves garlic
2/3 cups all-purpose flour
2 eggs
1/3 cup scallions
Salt and pepper, to taste
Cooking spray

1. Shred the zucchini and carrots, mince the garlic, and chop scallions using both the white and green portions.
2. Season the zucchini with salt, then press it in a colander, and let it sit for 10 minutes.
3. Use your hands to squeeze out as much liquid as possible from the zucchini.
4. Beat the eggs. Combine all the ingredients in a large bowl and mix well.
5. Spray your basket, then scoop small balls of the mixture into the basket giving them room to expand.
6. Spray the tops of the balls with oil.
7. Cook at 360°F for 10 minutes, flipping the fritters at the halfway point.

Nutrition
Calories: 144, Sodium: 76 mg, Dietary Fiber: 2.8 g, Fat: 2.5 g, Carbs: 24.5 g, Protein: 6.3 g.

Avocado Fries

These fries are so versatile, they can be used as a side, an appetizer, a snack, or even part of the main meal.

Servings: 4
Prep Time: 10 minutes
Cook Time: 10 minutes

1/2 cup all-purpose flour
1-1/2 teaspoons pepper
2 eggs
1 tablespoon water
1/2 cup panko
2 avocados
Cooking spray
1/4 teaspoon kosher salt

1. Cut the avocado into 8 wedges each.
2. Beat the eggs and water in a bowl. Combine the flour and pepper in another bowl.
3. Place the panko on a plate. Toss the avocado wedges in flour, dip them in egg, then dredge them through the panko.
4. Spray each wedge with cooking spray and transfer it to the basket.
5. Cook wedges in the air fryer at 390°F for 10 minutes, tossing at least once.
6. Sprinkle with salt and serve.

Nutrition

Calories: 349, Sodium: 284 mg, Dietary Fiber: 8 g, Fat: 22.7 g, Carbs: 31 g, Protein: 8.2 g.

Stuffed Mushrooms

Mushrooms are such a versatile food, and recipes like this prove that with a few simple ingredients you can create a fantastic appetizer or main dish.

Servings: 4
Prep Time: 15 minutes
Cook Time: 10 minutes

4 jumbo portobello mushrooms
1 tablespoon olive oil
1/4 cup ricotta cheese
5 tablespoons parmesan cheese
1 cup frozen chopped spinach, thawed
1/3 cup breadcrumbs
1/4 teaspoon fresh rosemary

1. Thaw and drain spinach. Mince rosemary.
2. Wipe the mushrooms with a damp cloth, remove stems, and hollow out inside.
3. Preheat the air fryer to 360°F.
4. Bake the mushrooms in your air fryer for 2 minutes.
5. Mix ricotta, 3 tablespoons parmesan cheese, spinach, breadcrumbs, and rosemary.
6. Remove mushrooms and drain any liquid that has accumulated in them.
7. Stuff mushrooms with the ricotta mixture and sprinkle the remaining parmesan on top.
8. Cook for another 6 - 8 minutes.

Nutrition

Calories: 135, Sodium: 197 mg, Dietary Fiber: 0.6 g, Fat: 7 g, Carbs: 9.8 g, Protein: 7.6 g.

Cheddar Biscuits

The air fryer isn't just about mimicking fried foods, it can also deliver perfectly baked appetizers like these scrumptious cheddar biscuits.

Servings: 8
Prep Time: 20 minutes
Cook Time: 20 minutes

2-1/3 cups self-rising flour
2 tablespoons sugar
1 stick butter
1/2 cup grated cheddar cheese
1-1/3 cups buttermilk
1 cup all-purpose flour
1 tablespoon melted butter

1. Freeze the butter for 15 minutes before starting.
2. Line a baking pan that fits in your air fryer with parchment paper.
3. Mix the self-rising flour and sugar in a bowl, then grate the butter into the same bowl.
4. Add the cheese to the same bowl and mix well. Add the buttermilk and stir until there are no streaks of flour.
5. Spread your all-purpose flour over a baking sheet.
6. Scoop out 8-10 small balls of dough and drop them on the floured cookie sheet. Be sure they don't touch.
7. Flour your hands, then coat the balls with flour, and toss them between your hands to dust off excess flour.
8. Preheat your air fryer to 380°F.
9. Place the dough balls in the baking pan packed next to each other. Brush with melted butter.
10. Cook in the air fryer for 20 minutes, checking a few times to make sure the biscuits aren't burning.
11. Let the basket cool before removing the pan.

Nutrition

Calories: 222, Sodium: 362 mg, Dietary Fiber: 20.8 g, Fat: 0.8 g, Carbs: 49.1 g, Protein: 13.7 g.

Fried Artichoke Hearts

This is another mouthwatering favorite that just so happens to be healthy. With salt and crunch, these artichoke hearts may be better than potato chips.

Servings: 6
Prep Time: 10 Minutes
Cook Time: 8 Minutes

14 water-packed artichoke hearts
1/2 cup all-purpose flour
1/4 teaspoon baking powder
Salt, to taste
6 tablespoons water
6 tablespoons panko breadcrumbs
1/4 teaspoon dried basil
1/4 teaspoon dried oregano
1/4 teaspoon paprika
1/4 teaspoon granulated garlic

1. Remove artichoke hearts from jar and lay them on a towel to dry.
2. Combine flour, baking powder, salt, and water in a shallow bowl. It should create a thick batter.
3. Combine the rest of your dry ingredients and mix well in a shallow bowl.
4. Dip the hearts in the batter allowing any extra to drip off.
5. Roll them in the breadcrumb mix.
6. Toss them in the air fryer and cook at 360°F for 8 minutes, flip once at the halfway point.

Nutrition

Calories: 222, Sodium: 362 mg, Dietary Fiber: 20.8 g, Fat: 0.8 g, Carbs: 49.1 g, Protein: 13.7 g.

Fried Pickles

This may be the easiest recipe in this book and it has a high yield making it a great party recipe. Guests will be surprised at how delicious these fried pickles are and you will feel happy knowing that you are serving an appetizer that is not dripping with fat.

Servings: 16
Prep Time: 5 minutes
Cook Time: 10 minutes

1 quart whole dill pickles
1 cup buttermilk
2 cups plain cornmeal
1 tablespoon sea salt

1. Remove the pickles from the jar and pat them down with a paper towel.
2. Quarter the pickles lengthwise.
3. Put the buttermilk in one bowl and mix together the cornmeal and salt in a separate bowl.
4. Dip each pickle in the butter milk, then roll it in the cornmeal mix until completely covered.
5. Using your air fryer, lay your pickles in a single layer in the basket and cook for 10 minutes at 320F, tossing them halfway through.

Nutrition

Calories: 66, Sodium: 841 mg, Dietary Fiber: 1.6 g, Total Fat: 0.8 g, Total Carbs: 13.3 g, Protein: 1.9 g.

Crispy Eggplant
Caprese Stacks

If you are looking to make a statement, look no further than this dish. It is just as much a work of art as it is an appetizer. It doesn't hurt that these flavors combined create a succulent starter.

Servings: 2
Prep Time: 10 minutes
Cook Time: 10 minutes

2 ripe tomatoes
1 (8-ounce) ball fresh mozzarella
6-8 leaves fresh basil
6 slices eggplant
1/4 cup flour
1 egg
1/2 cup panko breadcrumbs

1. Cut eggplant, tomatoes, and mozzarella each into 1/4 inch thick pieces.
2. Rinse the basil and pat it dry.
3. In 3 separate bowls pour flour, panko, and beat an egg.
4. Toss eggplant in flour, dip in egg, then toss in panko.
5. Cook in your air fryer at 320F for 10 minutes, flipping once.
6. Stack eggplant, tomato, mozzarella, and basil and serve.

Nutrition

Calories: 885, Sodium: 951 mg, Dietary Fiber: 51.6 g, Total Fat: 26.8 g, Total Carbs: 121.2 g, Protein: 55.0 g.

Crab Rangoon

Crab rangoon are a Chinese restaurant favorite due to their taste and texture. Now you can be the hero at your next house party, or on a random weeknight with how easy these are to make.

Servings: 4
Prep Time: 5 minutes
Cook Time: 10 minutes

- 5 ounces crabmeat
- 4 ounces cream cheese, room temperature
- 1 scallion, thinly sliced
- 1 clove garlic, finely chopped
- 1 teaspoon Worcestershire sauce
- 1/2 tablespoon toasted sesame oil
- Sea salt and freshly ground black pepper
- 12 wonton wrappers

1. Mix together all ingredients, except wrappers.
2. Roll out each of your wonton wrappers.
3. Drop in 1/2 teaspoon of crab mix in each wrapper.
4. Fold each wonton and place in the basket.
5. Cook at 400F in your air fryer for 10 minutes.

Nutrition

Calories: 431, Sodium: 946 mg, Dietary Fiber: 2 g, Total Fat: 13.2 g, Total Carbs: 62.4 g, Protein: 14.4 g.

Jalapeño Poppers

Jalapeño poppers may be the quintessential appetizer. This simple recipe will be the hit at any party or just as a special treat for the family. The best part is that it is easy and quick to make and just as quick to cook.

Servings: 4
Prep Time: 10 minutes
Cook Time: 10 minutes

- 12-18 whole fresh jalapeño
- 1 cup nonfat refried beans
- 1 cup shredded Monterey Jack or extra-sharp Cheddar cheese
- 1 scallion, sliced
- 1 teaspoon salt, divided
- 1/4 cup all-purpose flour
- 2 large eggs
- 1/2 cup fine cornmeal
- Olive oil or canola oil cooking spray

1. Start by slicing each jalapeño lengthwise on one side. Place the jalapeños side by side in a microwave safe bowl and microwave them until they are slightly soft; usually around 5 minutes.
2. While your jalapeños cook; mix refried beans, scallions, 1/2 teaspoon salt, and cheese in a bowl.
3. Once your jalapeños are softened you can scoop out the seeds and add one tablespoon of your refried bean mixture (It can be a little less if the pepper is smaller.) Press the jalapeño closed around the filling.
4. Beat your eggs in a small bowl and place your flour in a separate bowl. In a third bowl mix your cornmeal and the remaining salt. Roll each pepper in the flour, then dip it in the egg, and finally roll it in the cornmeal making sure to coat the entire pepper. Place the peppers on a flat surface and coat them with a cooking spray; olive oil cooking spray is suggested.
5. Cook in your air fryer at 400F for 5 minutes, turn each pepper, and then cook for another 5 minutes; serve hot.

Nutrition

Calories: 244, Sodium: 800 mg, Dietary Fiber: 2.4 g, Total Fat: 12.5 g, Total Carbs: 20.7 g, Protein: 12.8 g.

CHAPTER 6

Poultry Dishes

Sweet & Spicy Firecracker Chicken

This dish is for the adventurous in your household. If you can handle a little heat, the sweet will make it worth your while.

Servings: 4
Prep Time: 10 minutes
Cook Time: 35 minutes

- 1/2 cup packed light brown sugar
- 1/3 cup buffalo sauce
- 1 tablespoon apple cider vinegar
- 1/4 teaspoon salt
- 1/4 teaspoon red pepper flakes
- 1 lb. boneless skinless chicken breast
- 1/2 cup cornstarch
- 2 large eggs

1. Start by cutting the chicken breast into 1 inch cubes.
2. In a large bowl, mix buffalo sauce, apple cider vinegar, salt, and red pepper flakes.
3. Place the cornstarch in a plastic container or bag.
4. Beat the eggs in a bowl.
5. Toss the chicken in the cornstarch, then dip it in egg.
6. Cook chicken in your air fryer at 360F for about 5 minutes; the chicken does not need to be fully cooked, only crisp on the outside.
7. Place the chicken in a baking pan and pour the buffalo sauce mixture over it. Return to air fryer.
8. Continue to bake at 350F for 30 minutes.

Nutrition

Calories: 385.5, Sodium: 2720 mg, Dietary Fiber: 2.5 g, Total Fat: 6.6 g, Total Carbs: 37.7 g, Protein: 39.7 g.

Fried Chicken
Livers

Most people shudder at the idea of liver but this recipe will have them changing their tune. This dish is super easy to make and about as delicious as they come.

Servings: 4
Prep Time: 5 minutes
Cook Time: 10 minutes

1 lb. chicken livers
1 cup flour
1/2 cup cornmeal
2 teaspoons herbs de provence
3 eggs
2 tablespoons milk

1. Clean and rinse the livers, pat dry.
2. Beat eggs in a shallow bowl and mix in milk.
3. In another bowl combine flour, cornmeal, and seasoning, mixing until even.
4. Dip the livers in the egg mix, then toss them in the flour mix.
5. Air fry at 375F for 10 minutes. Toss at least once halfway through.

Nutrition
Calories: 409, Sodium: 142 mg, Dietary Fiber: 2.0 g, Total Fat: 11.7 g, Total Carbs: 37.2 g, Protein: 36.6 g.

Chicken Parmesan

Chicken parmesan is a fantastic family favorite that is made healthy and even crunchier by cooking it in an air fryer.

Servings: 4
Prep Time: 10 minutes
Cook Time: 10 minutes

2 (8 ounce) chicken breast
6 tablespoons seasoned breadcrumbs
2 tablespoons parmesan cheese
1 tablespoon olive oil
6 tablespoons mozzarella cheese
1/2 cup marinara sauce
Cooking spray

1. Cut the chicken in half vertically to create 4 breasts.
2. Mix the breadcrumbs and parmesan together in a bowl.
3. Brush the chicken with olive oil.
4. Press the chicken into the breadcrumb mix.
5. Preheat the air fryer to 360°F.
6. Place 2 chicken breasts in the basket and spray with cooking spray.
7. Cook for 6 minutes.
8. Flip the chicken and top with 1 tablespoon marinara and 1 - 1/2 tablespoons mozzarella.
9. Cook for 3 more minutes, then repeat with the other 2 breasts.

Nutrition

Calories: 250, Sodium: 565 mg, Dietary Fiber: 1.1 g, Fat: 14.8 g, Carbs: 11.4 g, Protein: 18.8 g

Turkey
with Maple Mustard Glaze

Doesn't the name by itself just make your mouth water? This recipe is sure to please the whole family any day of the year.

Servings: 4
Prep Time: 10 minutes
Cook Time: 50 minutes

2 teaspoons olive oil
3 lbs. whole turkey breast
1 teaspoon dried thyme
1/2 teaspoon dried sage
1/2 teaspoon smoked paprika
1 teaspoon salt
1/2 teaspoon black pepper
1/4 cup maple syrup
2 tablespoons Dijon mustard
1 tablespoon butter

1. Preheat the air fryer to 350°F. Brush the entire turkey breast with olive oil.
2. Combine dry seasonings and toss to mix.
3. Rub the seasonings over the turkey and put it in the air fryer, frying for 25 minutes.
4. Turn it on one side and fry for another 12 minutes. Turn it on the other side and cook for 12 more minutes.
5. Melt the butter in a bowl and mix in syrup and mustard.
6. Return the turkey to its upright position and brush the syrup mix over the turkey.
7. Cook for 5 more minutes before serving.

Nutrition
Calories: 404, Sodium: 218 mg, Dietary Fiber: 0.6 g, Fat: 8.1 g, Carbs: 14.2 g, Protein: 58 g.

Buttermilk
Fried Chicken

There are very few people in this world that will be able to resist this delicious buttermilk fried chicken recipe! And why should they? It's much healthier than traditional chicken fried in oil.

Servings: 6
Prep Time: 10 minutes
Cook Time: 18 minutes

1-1/2 lbs. chicken thighs
2 cups buttermilk
2 teaspoons salt
2 teaspoons black pepper
1 teaspoon cayenne pepper
2 cups all-purpose flour
1 tablespoon baking powder
1 tablespoon garlic powder
1 tablespoon paprika powder

1. Rinse chicken pieces and pat dry.
2. Put chicken pieces in a bowl and add salt, pepper, and cayenne, tossing to cover.
3. Pour the buttermilk over the chicken and refrigerate for at least 6 hours.
4. Combine flour, baking powder, paprika, and garlic powder and stir to combine evenly.
5. Preheat the air fryer to 350°F.
6. Pull the chicken out one piece at a time and toss in the flour mix.
7. Working in batches, cook them in the air fryer for 8 minutes on one side, then 10 minutes on the other.

Nutrition
Calories: 413, Sodium: 963mg, Dietary Fiber: 2 g, Fat: 9.8 g, Carbs: 39.2 g, Protein: 40.3 g

Chicken Fajita Roll Ups

The only thing better than a good chicken fajita is being able to cook this imaginative meal in your kitchen.

Servings: 6
Prep Time: 25 minutes
Cook Time: 12 minutes

3 chicken breasts
1/2 red, green, and yellow bell pepper
1/2 red onion
2 teaspoons paprika
1 teaspoon garlic powder
1 teaspoon cumin powder
1/2 teaspoon cayenne
1/2 teaspoon oregano
Salt and pepper, to taste
Cooking spray
Toothpicks

1. Cut the bell pepper halves vertically into thin strips.
2. Mix together all of your spices.
3. Cut into half each chicken breast through the middle.
4. Pound each breast half flat.
5. Season both sides of each piece of chicken with the spice blend.
6. Place 2 bell pepper strips of each color and a few pieces of onion in the center of each piece of chicken.
7. Roll the chicken up around the peppers and onions and use 1 or 2 toothpicks to hold the roll up shut.
8. Preheat your air fryer to 390°F.
9. Spray each roll up with cooking spray and cook 3 at a time for 12 minutes.

Nutrition

Calories: 70, Sodium: 27 mg, Dietary Fiber: 0.8 g, Fat: 1.5 g, Carbs: 2.7 g, Protein: 11.1 g.

Crispy Coconut Chicken

A good coconut chicken is welcome any time of year, but I especially like to cook it in the summer, so I can imagine I'm on a tropical vacation.

Servings: 4
Prep Time: 15 minutes
Cook Time: 15 minutes

- 1/2 cup cornstarch
- 1/4 teaspoon salt
- 1/8 teaspoon pepper
- 3 eggs
- 2 cups sweetened coconut flakes
- 2 cups unsweetened coconut flakes
- 4 medium boneless chicken breasts

1. Beat the eggs and cut the chicken into strips.
2. Mix cornstarch, salt, and pepper in a separate bowl.
3. Place your sweetened and unsweetened coconut in a third shallow bowl or plate; mix well.
4. Roll the chicken in the cornstarch mix.
5. Dip the chicken in the egg, then roll it in coconut.
6. Preheat the air fryer to 360°F.
7. Cook for 15 minutes, flipping halfway through.

Calories: 452, Sodium: 248 mg, Dietary Fiber: 7.4 g, Fat: 30.8 g, Carbs: 27.1 g, Protein: 19.9 g.

Tandoori Chicken

You can't go wrong with this amazing Indian inspired recipe that is the perfect dinner on endless summer nights.

Servings: 4
Prep Time: 25 minutes + 10 hours
Cook Time: 30 minutes

- 4 chicken legs
- 3 teaspoons ginger paste
- 3 teaspoons garlic paste
- Salt, to taste
- 3 tablespoons lemon juice
- 2 tablespoon tandoori masala powder
- 1 teaspoon roasted cumin powder
- 1 teaspoon garam masala powder
- 2 teaspoons red chili powder
- 1 teaspoon turmeric powder
- 4 tablespoons hung curd
- 2 teaspoons kasoori methi
- 1 teaspoon black pepper
- 2 teaspoons coriander powder

1. Wash the chicken legs and cut a few slits in each one. Mix ginger paste, garlic paste, and salt together.
2. Put chicken in a bowl and coat with the ginger paste mix. Set the chicken in the fridge for 15 minutes.
3. While the chicken marinates, mix all the other ingredients together.
4. Pour the marinade over the chicken and return to the fridge for at least 10 hours.
5. Preheat the air fryer to 360°F. Cook the chicken for 30 minutes, turning halfway through.

Nutrition

Calories: 186, Sodium: 347 mg, Dietary Fiber: 1.2 g, Fat: 12.5 g, Carbs: 5.3 g, Protein: 13.4 g.

Homemade Chicken Nuggets

You can't go wrong with chicken nuggets and when you make them yourself, you know exactly what goes into them.

Servings: 4
Prep Time: 10 minutes
Cook Time: 10 minutes

- 2 (8 ounce) skinless boneless chicken breasts, cut into nugget sized pieces
- Salt and pepper, to taste
- 2 teaspoons olive oil
- 6 tablespoons Italian seasoned breadcrumbs
- 2 tablespoons panko breadcrumbs
- 2 tablespoons parmesan cheese
- Olive oil spray

1. Put chicken, olive oil, salt, and pepper in a bowl and toss to coat.
2. Mix the breadcrumbs and parmesan together in a bowl.
3. Toss the chicken in the breadcrumb mixture.
4. Place the chicken in the basket and spray with olive oil spray.
5. Preheat the air fryer to 390°F.
6. Cook for 10 minutes, tossing halfway through.

Nutrition

Calories: 338, Sodium: 362 mg, Dietary Fiber: 0.8 g, Fat: 9.4 g, Carbs: 9.7 g, Protein: 50.5 g.

Buffalo Chicken Meatballs

If you love buffalo wings, then you will adore these meatballs! They taste great on their own or in a meatball sub sandwich.

Servings: 4
Prep Time: 10 minutes
Cook Time: 10 minutes

1 lb. ground chicken
4 garlic cloves
1 package ranch seasoning
1 cup seasoned breadcrumbs
1 cup hot sauce
1 cup ranch dressing
1/2 cup blue cheese crumbles

1. Mince the garlic.
2. Combine garlic, ranch seasoning, and breadcrumbs in a large bowl.
3. Add the chicken and knead the ingredients together.
4. Roll into small balls.
5. Cook for 360°F for 5 minutes using the air fryer.
6. Toss the meatballs in the hot sauce and cook for another 5 minutes.
7. Mix together ranch and blue cheese crumbles.
8. Drizzle ranch mix over meatballs before serving.

Nutrition
Calories: 326, Sodium: 233 mg, Dietary Fiber: 0.6 g, Fat: 13.7 g, Carbs: 10.5 g, Protein: 37.7 g.

Chicken Wontons

This is a great versatile recipe that can be used as the side to a meal, an appetizer, or as the main dish. Add a crisp salad and you've got an incomparable dinner!

Servings: 4
Prep Time: 25 minutes
Cook Time: 12 minutes

- 1 cup all-purpose flour
- 1/4 lb. boneless skinless chicken breast
- 1 egg
- 1 green onion
- 1 tablespoon French beans
- 1 tablespoon carrots
- 1/2 teaspoon pepper powder
- 1/4 teaspoon soy sauce
- 1/2 teaspoon cornstarch
- 1 teaspoon sesame seed oil

1. Finely dice all of your vegetables, beans, and chicken into the smallest pieces possible.
2. Mix flour, salt, and a little hot water to create a stiff dough. Cover and set aside.
3. Beat the egg in a large bowl. Add all other ingredients, except for the sesame seed oil, to the egg bowl and mix well.
4. Add the sesame seed oil to the mix and mix again.
5. Roll your dough flat and use a cookie cutter to cut it into circles about 6 inches in diameter. You can also use pre-made wonton wrappers.
6. Preheat the air fryer to 360°F. Scoop a little mixture into the center of each circle.
7. Use your fingers to wet the edges of the circles. Fold them over the stuffing and press to close. Cook in the fryer for 12 minutes, flipping them after 7 minutes.

Nutrition

Calories: 185, Sodium: 51 mg, Dietary Fiber: 1.7 g, Fat: 3.3 g, Carbs: 26.6 g, Protein: 11.3 g.

Chicken
Kabobs

These chicken kabobs are an excellent way to take advantage of the skewers that come with your air fryer. Try them in pita bread with harissa sauce.

Servings: 2
Prep Time: 15 minutes
Cook Time: 20 minutes

2 chicken breasts
1/3 cup honey
1/3 cup soy sauce
Sesame seeds
6 mushrooms
1 each- red, yellow, and green bell pepper
Cooking spray
Salt, to taste

1. Cut the chicken breast into cubes.
2. Spray the cubes with cooking spray and season with salt and pepper.
3. Transfer to a bowl and mix chicken with honey, soy sauce, and sesame seeds.
4. Cut mushrooms in half.
5. Preheat your air fryer to 340°F.
6. Add chicken, peppers, and mushrooms onto the skewers, alternating each one until the skewers are full.
7. Cook in the air fryer for 20 minutes, turning the kabobs at the halfway mark.

Nutrition
Calories: 377, Sodium: 245 mg, Dietary Fiber: 3.4 g, Fat: 3.1 g, Carbs: 65.1 g, Protein: 27.5 g.

CHAPTER

7

Beef, Lamb
& Pork Dishes

Cheese Burger Eggrolls

These eggrolls make it easy to take your cheese burger on the go and cooking them in the air fryer makes the outside crisp and the inside juicy.

Servings: 14
Prep Time: 20 minutes
Cook Time: 12 minutes

1 lb. ground beef
1/2 yellow onion
1 tablespoon vegetable oil for cooking
5 ounces cheddar cheese, grated
1/2 cup pickles
14 egg roll wrappers
1 egg
Salt and pepper, to taste

1. Heat the oil in a pan. Dice the onion and the pickles into small pieces. Sauté the onions 3 - 4 minutes. Add ground beef and brown, draining off any extra fat.
2. Transfer the beef mixture to a bowl and break up the cheese slices into the bowl.
3. Add the pickles and mix the cheese and pickles into the mixture.
4. Separate the egg in a separate bowl and discard the yolk.
5. Roll out the eggrolls and spoon an even amount of the beef mixture into the center of each egg roll.
6. Wet the edges of the wrappers with egg whites. Pull the bottom left corner of the wrapper over the mixture, then fold each side in.
7. Roll the eggrolls to close, then place them in your basket.
8. Using the air fryer, cook at 390°F for 10 minutes, flipping halfway through.

Nutrition

Calories: 193, Sodium: 371 mg, Dietary Fiber: 0.7 g, Fat: 5.7 g, Carbs: 19.6 g, Protein: 14.8 g.

Roasted Stuffed Peppers

Add some fun and flair to supper time with these easy to make stuffed peppers that taste as good as they look.

Servings: 2
Prep Time: 15 minutes
Cook Time: 20 minutes

2 green peppers
1/2 onion
1 garlic clove
1 teaspoon olive oil
1/2 lb. ground beef
1/2 cup tomato sauce
1 teaspoon Worcestershire sauce
1/2 teaspoon salt
1/2 teaspoon black pepper
4 ounces shredded cheddar cheese

1. Salt a pot of water and heat on high.
2. Remove the stems and seeds from the green peppers.
3. Boil the green pepper shells for 3 minutes.
4. Mince the garlic clove and dice the onion.
5. Heat the olive oil in a pan, then add onion and garlic to sauté.
6. Add the ground beef to the pan and cook until browned.
7. Transfer the beef to a bowl and mix in sauces, half of the cheese, salt, and pepper.
8. Preheat the air fryer to 390°F.
9. Stuff each pepper with the beef mix and top with the remaining cheese.
10. Put the peppers in the basket and cook for 20 minutes.

Nutrition

Calories: 515, Sodium: 1362 mg, Dietary Fiber: 3.7 g, Fat: 28.6 g, Carbs: 13.5 g, Protein: 50.8 g.

Country Fried Steak

Country fried steak is a southern staple and this air fryer recipe combined with the super simple white gravy is an absolute treat.

Servings: 1
Prep Time: 20 minutes
Cook Time 12 minutes

6 ounces sirloin steak
3 eggs
1 cup flour
1 cup panko
1 teaspoon onion powder
1 teaspoon garlic powder
1 teaspoon salt
1 teaspoon pepper

Gravy:

1/2 lb. ground sausage
2 tablespoons flour
2 cups milk
1 teaspoon pepper

1. Pound the steak thin.
2. Beat the eggs in a bowl.
3. Put the flour on a plate.
4. Mix the panko, onion powder, garlic powder, salt, and pepper together in a shallow bowl.
5. Preheat your air fryer to 360°F.
6. Press the steak into the flour, dip in egg, and toss it in the panko mix to cover completely.
7. Place the steak in the basket cooking for 12 minutes, flipping halfway through.
8. While the steak cooks, brown the sausage on the stove.
9. Drain most of the fat, then mix in the flour.
10. Add the milk and pepper and mix until it forms a thick gravy.
11. Pour the gravy over the steak and serve.

Nutrition

Calories: 687, Sodium: 311 mg, Dietary Fiber: 2.5 g, Fat: 20.1 g, Carbs: 42.4 g, Protein: 80.8 g.

Chinese Beef Spare Ribs

As if spare ribs weren't good enough, this recipe takes them to the next level while keeping them relatively healthy.

Servings: 4
Prep Time: 40 minutes
Cook Time: 8 minutes

- 1 tablespoon sesame oil
- 1 teaspoon minced garlic
- 1 teaspoon minced ginger
- 1 tablespoon fermented black bean paste
- 1 tablespoon Shaoxing wine
- 1 tablespoon dark soy sauce
- 1 tablespoon honey
- 1-1/2 lbs. beef spareribs

1. Cut the spare ribs into small pieces.
2. Mix all of the ingredients together in a bowl and add spare ribs.
3. Refrigerate the ribs for 30 minutes.
4. Preheat the air fryer to 375°F.
5. Place them in the basket and cook for 8 minutes, shaking halfway through.

Nutrition

Calories: 579, Sodium: 474 mg, Dietary Fiber: 0.3 g, Fat: 36.3 g, Carbs: 5.7 g, Protein: 53.6 g.

Air Fryer Burgers

After trying one of these delicious air fryer burgers, you'll forget all about the grill!

Servings: 4
Prep Time: 10 minutes
Cook Time: 10 minutes

1 lb. ground beef
1 tablespoon Worcestershire sauce
Liquid smoke
1/2 teaspoon garlic powder
1/2 teaspoon onion powder
1/2 teaspoon salt
1/2 teaspoon black pepper

1. Mix together the Worcestershire sauce, seasonings, and a few drops of liquid smoke in a small bowl.
2. In a larger bowl, knead the Worcestershire sauce spice mixture and beef together until well blended.
3. Split the burger into 4 even sized patties and flatten.
4. Preheat the air fryer to 350°F and place the patties in the basket.
5. For a medium burger, cook for 10 minutes, flipping halfway through.

Nutrition

Calories: 217, Sodium: 407 mg, Dietary Fiber: 0.1 g, Fat: 7.1 g, Carbs: 1.4 g, Protein: 34.5 g.

Steak Roll Ups

These steak roll ups break the dinner monotony by combining yummy steak with pesto and cheese in one mouthwatering tube of flavor!

Servings: 2
Prep Time: 10 minutes
Cook Time: 15 minutes

2 (8 ounce) Flank Steaks
2 tablespoons pesto
4 slices cheddar cheese
1 red bell pepper, sliced
1/2 cup baby spinach
1 teaspoon sea salt
1 teaspoon pepper

1. Tenderize the meat and flatten it a little more.
2. Spread the pesto over one side of each steak and sprinkle with salt and pepper.
3. Layer the cheese, pepper, and spinach over the steak.
4. Preheat the air fryer to 390°F.
5. Roll each steak up as tight as you can and secure it with toothpicks.
6. Cook in the fryer for 15 minutes, flipping once halfway through.

Nutrition

Calories: 757, Sodium: 1514 mg, Dietary Fiber: 1.5 g, Fat: 44.1 g, Carbs: 7.2 g, Protein: 79.5 g.

Coffee & Chili Rub Steak

You'll feel like a professional chef when you pull off this impressive recipe inspired by Gordon Ramsey.

Servings: 4
Prep Time: 20 minutes
Cook Time: 20 minutes

4 boneless ribeye steaks
1/4 cup ancho chili powder
1/4 cup espresso powder
2 tablespoons paprika
2 tablespoons brown sugar
1 tablespoon dry mustard
1 tablespoon kosher salt
1 tablespoon black pepper
1 tablespoon ground coriander
1 tablespoon dried oregano
2 teaspoons ginger
2 teaspoons Aleppo pepper
Salt and pepper, to taste

1. Combine all of the spices in a bowl and mix well.
2. Preheat the air fryer to 390°F.
3. Press each side of each steak into the spice mixture until well coated.
4. Cook the steaks, one at a time, for 20 minutes a piece, flipping halfway through.

Nutrition

Calories: 341, Sodium: 843 mg, Dietary Fiber: 2.7 g, Fat: 16.4 g, Carbs: 11.8 g, Protein: 38.7 g.

Marinated Beef Tips

These beef tips are full of flavor and easy to combine with pasta, rice, or vegetables.

Servings: 4
Prep Time: 40 minutes
Cook Time: 10 minutes

1 lb. sirloin beef tips
2 tablespoons olive oil
1/4 cup green onions
3 tablespoons flour
1/2 tablespoon garlic salt
1/2 teaspoon black pepper
1 cup beef broth
1/2 cup red wine
1 can cream of mushroom soup

1. Combine all marinade ingredients except beef, flour, and onions in a large bowl.
2. Toss the beef tips in the flour and then place them in the bowl with the marinade. Refrigerate for 30 minutes.
3. Chop the green onions and transfer to a bowl.
4. When the beef is done marinating, add it to the onion bowl and toss to season with onion.
5. Using the air fryer, cook beef tips in the basket for 10 minutes, tossing once halfway through.

Nutrition

Calories: 406, Sodium: 665 mg, Dietary Fiber: 0.5 g, Fat: 17.7 g, Carbs: 11.8 g, Protein: 45.3 g.

Crispy Fried Pork Cutlets

This is an easy way to take an already tasty dish and make it even better. Crispy pork is not as common as it should be because the crispy outside really takes pork cutlets to the next level.

Servings: 4
Prep Time: 10 minutes
Cook Time: 14 minutes

1-1/2 cups panko bread crumbs
1/2 cup grated parmesan
Sea salt
1 lb. pork tenderloin, sliced 3/4 inches thick, pounded 1/4 inch thick
2 eggs

1. Beat the eggs in a shallow bowl and set aside.
2. In a separate bowl mix together panko, 1/2 teaspoon salt, and parmesan; once completely mixed pour on to a plate.
3. Dip the pork cutlets in egg, then press into panko mix on each side to coat evenly.
4. Cook at 360F for 14 minutes, flipping halfway through.

Nutrition

Calories: 2,745, Sodium: 3160 mg, Dietary Fiber: 1.8 g, Total Fat: 97.7 g, Total Carbs: 37.4 g, Protein: 414.9 g.

Meatloaf

Meatloaf has been a family staple for years and now you can make it in your air fryer for an even better texture and flavor.

Servings: 4
Prep Time: 10 minutes
Cook Time: 25 minutes

1 lb. ground beef
1/8 cup chili sauce
1 dry onion soup packet
1/8 cup Worcestershire sauce
1/2 cup Italian style breadcrumbs
1/4 cup water
2 tablespoons milk
Salt and pepper, to taste

1. Preheat your air fryer to 390°F.
2. Mix together all of the ingredients, except for the chili sauce and put into two mini bread pans.
3. Pour a little chili sauce over each loaf.
4. Cook each loaf for 25 minutes in the fryer and allow to cool for 10 minutes before serving.

Nutrition

Calories: 280, Sodium: 615 mg, Dietary Fiber: 0.8 g, Fat: 8.1 g, Carbs: 12.3 g, Protein: 36.8 g.

Bacon Cheeseburger Bombs

We call these 'bombs' because they explode with flavor in your mouth!

Servings: 5
Prep Time: 20 minutes
Cook Time: 15 minutes

1 can refrigerated biscuits
1 lb. ground beef
1/2 onion
3 slices of bacon
1/3 cup cream cheese
1 tablespoon ketchup
2 tablespoons barbecue sauce
1 teaspoon yellow mustard
1 teaspoon Worcestershire sauce
3 cheddar cheese slices
1 egg
Sesame seeds

1. Chop up the bacon and onions.
2. In a large skillet cook the onions, bacon, and beef until bacon and beef are browned.
3. Add the Worcestershire, mustard, barbeque, ketchup, and cream cheese to the skillet and stir until cream cheese is completely melted.
4. Cut the cheese slices into quarters.
5. Separate the biscuits and roll each one out flat.
6. Place 1 cheese quarter in the center of each biscuit, then spoon even amounts of the beef mixture over each square.
7. Fold the biscuit around the mixture, pressing it together in the center to close.
8. Separate the egg in a bowl and discard the yolk.
9. Brush each biscuit with egg whites and sprinkle with sesame seeds.
10. Preheat the air fryer to 375°F.
11. Cook in the fryer for 15 minutes, flipping the bombs halfway through.

Nutrition

Calories: 423, Sodium: 566 mg, Dietary Fiber: 0.4 g, Fat: 26 g, Carbs: 8.4 g, Protein: 37.2 g.

Bacon Wrapped Hot Dog

By themselves, bacon and especially hot dogs, aren't anything spectacular, but when you combine the two and put them in an air fryer, they will make your taste buds sing.

Servings: 2
Prep Time: 5 minutes
Cook Time: 10 minutes

2 beef hotdogs
2 strips of bacon
2 hotdog buns
Your favorite garnishes

1. Preheat the air fryer to 390°F.
2. Wrap a slice of bacon around each hot dog.
3. Cook the hotdogs in the fryer for 8 minutes, turning every 2 minutes or so.
4. Reduce heat to 360°F and remove hotdogs. Bacon should be crisp.
5. Put the hot dogs in the buns and return to the fryer for another minute or so.
6. Top with condiments and serve while the bun is still warm.

Nutrition

Calories: 422, Sodium: 881 mg, Dietary Fiber: 0.9 g, Fat: 28.4 g, Carbs: 22.6 g, Protein: 16.4 g.

Air Fryer Strip Steak

Sometimes simple is just better, as this four-ingredient strip steak recipe proves.

Servings: 1
Prep Time: 3 minutes
Cook Time 12 minutes

1 strip steak
1 teaspoon olive oil
Salt and pepper, to taste

1. Use a meat tenderizer to tenderize the steak.
2. Preheat your air fryer to 390°F.
3. Brush each side of the steak with olive oil and season with salt and pepper.
4. Cook for 12 minutes, flipping halfway through.

Nutrition

Calories: 190, Sodium: 70 mg, Dietary Fiber: 0 g, Fat: 9.7 g, Carbs: 0 g, Protein: 0 g.

Adobo Crusted Lamb Loin Chops

Lamb is a rich meat with its own distinct flavor and recipes like this one really help to bring it out. The delicious herb blend complements the savory aspect of the dish.

Servings: 4
Prep Time: 1 hr 10 minutes
Cook Time: 15 minutes

1 tablespoon fennel seed
1 tablespoon cumin seed
2 teaspoons coriander seed
2 teaspoons cracked pepper
1-1/2 teaspoons salt
2 teaspoons minced garlic cloves
2 teaspoons fresh oregano leaves
2 teaspoons lime zest
1/2 teaspoon fresh thyme
1/2 teaspoon fresh rosemary leaves
8 lamb loin chops, 1-inch thick

1. Throw fennel, cumin, coriander, and pepper in a dry skillet and cook on medium heat until aromatic.
2. Let cool then grind in a spice grinder or mortar.
3. Put ground mix into a bowl and mix in salt, lime zest, oregano, and garlic.
4. Next, mix in rosemary and thyme.
5. Rub each side of the lamb chop with the spice mix then cover and set in the fridge for one hour.
6. Cook at 360F for 15 minutes, flipping half way through.

Nutrition

Calories: 751, Sodium: 1161 mg, Dietary Fiber: 1.6 g, Total Fat: 32.7 g, Total Carbs: 3.5 g, Protein: 100.8 g.

Roast Beef

Have ever questioned how amazing cooking with an air fryer can be? The fact that you can make a whole roast beef to perfection should clear up any doubts.

Servings: 6
Prep Time: 10 minutes
Cook Time: 40 minutes

3 lbs. top round roast
2 teaspoons olive oil
1 teaspoon salt
1/4 teaspoon black pepper
1 teaspoon dried thyme
1/2 teaspoon rosemary

1. Mix salt, pepper, thyme, and rosemary.
2. Brush the roast on all sides with olive oil.
3. Preheat the air fryer to 360°F.
4. Rub the roast on all sides with the spice mixture.
5. Cook for 40 minutes, rotating the roast every 10 minutes or so for even cooking.

Nutrition
Calories: 502, Sodium: 526 mg, Dietary Fiber: 0.2 g, Fat: 21.7 g, Carbs: 0.3 g, Protein: 71.9 g.

Lamb Kofta Kabobs

This Middle Eastern dish is amazing and can easily be used as an appetizer or a main course. It also gives you a chance to have some fun and use the skewers that come with your air fryer.

Servings: 4
Prep Time: 15 minutes
Cook Time: 10 minutes

1 tablespoon coriander seeds
1 tablespoon cumin seeds
1 teaspoon peppercorns
1 teaspoon allspice
1/2 teaspoon cardamom seeds
1/2 teaspoon turmeric powder
1 tablespoon oil
1 lb. ground lamb
1/4 cup parsley
1 tablespoon minced garlic

1. Grind the seeds and peppercorns into powder and combine with the turmeric and allspice.
2. Combine all of the ingredients together in a blender and blend until well mixed.
3. Divide the meat into 4 equal parts and form a sausage around the skewers.
4. Cook in the air fryer at 370°F for 10 minutes.

Nutrition
Calories: 255, Sodium: 81 mg, Dietary Fiber: 0.7 g, Fat: 11 g, Carbs: 2.6 g, Protein: 35.1 g.

Tuscan Pork Chops

Pork is not a traditional Mediterranean dish, but this recipe combines the flavors of Tuscany with the 'other white meat'. This recipe is super simple for an Italian dish and offers rich and delicious flavor to be served with pasta or grilled vegetables!

Servings: 4
Prep Time: 10 minutes
Cook Time: 20 minutes

1/4 cup all-purpose flour
1 teaspoon salt
3/4 teaspoon seasoned pepper
4 (1-inch-thick) boneless pork chops
1 tablespoon olive oil
3 to 4 garlic cloves
1/3 cup balsamic vinegar
1/3 cup chicken broth
3 plum tomatoes, seeded and diced
2 tablespoons capers

1. Combine flour, salt, and pepper
2. Press pork chops into flour mixture on both sides until evenly covered.
3. Cook in your air fryer at 360F for 14 minutes, flipping halfway through.
4. While the pork chops cook, warm olive oil in a medium skillet.
5. Add garlic and sauté for 1 minute; then mix in vinegar and chicken broth.
6. Add capers and tomatoes and turn to high heat.
7. Bring the sauce to a boil, stirring regularly, then add pork chops, cooking for one minute.
8. Remove from heat and cover for about 5 minutes to allow the pork to absorb some of the sauce; serve hot.

Nutrition

Calories: 349, Sodium: 842 mg, Dietary Fiber: 1.5 g, Total Fat: 23.8 g, Total Carbs: 12.3 g, Protein: 20.6 g.

Asian Pork Chops

These sweet pork chops are a nice change from the usual mustard-marinated pork chop recipes that everyone loves. Sweet and savory, these are delicious with just about any vegetable side dish and steamed rice.

Servings: 4
Prep Time: 2 hrs 10 minutes
Cook Time: 15 minutes

1/2 cup Hoisin sauce
3 tablespoons cider vinegar
1 tablespoon sweet chili sauce
1/4 teaspoon garlic powder
4 (1/2-inch-thick) boneless pork chops
1 teaspoon salt
1/2 teaspoon pepper

1. Stir together Hoisin, chili sauce, garlic powder, and vinegar in a large mixing bowl.
2. Separate 1/4 cup of this mixture, then add pork chops to the bowl and marinate in the fridge for 2 hours.
3. Remove the pork chops and place them on a plate.
4. Sprinkle each side of the pork chop evenly with salt and pepper.
5. Cook at 360F for 14 minutes, flipping halfway through.
6. Brush with reserved marinade and serve.

Nutrition

Calories: 338, Sodium: 1185 mg, Dietary Fiber: 1.0 g, Total Fat: 21 g, Total Carbs: 16 g, Protein: 19.1 g.

Simple Fried Pork Chops

Sometimes simple is better, and these pork chops are an excellent example. They are not overstated, but taste great and can be paired with almost any side dish for a relatively quick and easy dinner.

Servings: 4
Prep Time: 1 hour 5 minutes
Cook Time: 14 minutes

4 thick slices pork chops
2 teaspoons sea salt
1 teaspoon ground black pepper
2 teaspoons garlic powder

1. Mix salt, pepper, and garlic powder in a bowl.
2. Press the pork chops into the mixture until evenly coated then set aside for 1 hour.
3. Cook in your air fryer at 360F for 14 minutes, flipping halfway through.

Nutrition
Calories: 262, Sodium: 1219 mg, Dietary Fiber: 0 g, Total Fat: 19.9 g, Total Carbs: 1.4 g, Protein: 18.3 g.

CHAPTER 8

Seafood

Fried Squid
with Aioli

Fried squid is one of those delicious taste sensations that are so easy to eat. With the crispy coating and the tender inside, you won't be able to eat just one. Plus; how often do you have a chance to make your own aioli?

Servings: 4
Prep Time: 40 minutes
Cook Time: 10 minutes

2/3 cup potato starch
1-1/4 teaspoons baking powder
1-3/4 cups arepa flour
1 large egg yolk
1 garlic clove, finely grated
1 teaspoon fresh lemon juice
1/2 cup grapeseed oil
1/4 cup olive oil
Sea salt
6 ounces cleaned squid, bodies and tentacles separated
4 scallions, white and pale-green parts only, sliced into 3-inch pieces
4 very thin lemon wheels
1/3 cup torn basil leaves

1. In a large bowl, mix the 3/4 cup arepa flour, baking powder, and potato starch together.
2. Mix 2-1/3 cups water into the arepa flour mix and allow it to sit for half an hour.
3. Place the remaining arepa flour in a separate shallow bowl.
4. While the arepa flour mix is hydrating mix the egg yolk, lemon juice, and garlic in a separate bowl.
5. Continue to stir the egg yolk mix while slowly pouring in the grapeseed and olive oils. Keep stirring until the sauce thickens – this is your aioli.
6. Season the aioli with salt and add a teaspoon of water to make it ready to serve.
7. Cut your squid into triangular chunks that are about 1/2-inch wide at the bottom.
8. Rinse the chunks and pat them down with a dry paper towel.
9. Coat the squid, lemon slices, and scallions in the plain arepa flour and then in the arepa flour batter mix.
10. Cook them in batches in your air fryer at 360F for about 10 minutes, tossing half way through.
11. Top with basil and serve with your homemade aioli sauce.

Calories: 945, Sodium: 33 mg, Dietary Fiber: 3.9 g, Total Fat: 42.7 g, Total Carbs: 121.3 g, Protein: 18.2 g.

Fried
Scallops

Scallops are a delicious treat when air fried. This recipe is super simple, super quick, and yields many servings making it a great option for party fare.

Servings: 12
Prep Time: 5 minutes
Cook Time: 10 minutes

1. Combine flour, corn flour, and baking power in a medium bowl.
2. Pat scallops dry, then toss in flour mix.
3. Cook in air fryer at 375F for 10 minutes, shaking a few times. Serve with a squeeze of lemon juice.

1 cup white flour
1 cup fine corn meal
1 teaspoon baking powder
4 lbs. scallops, under 10 to 12 to a lb., preferably dry
Lemon wedges

Nutrition
Calories: 211, Sodium: 244 mg, Dietary Fiber: 1.3 g, Total Fat: 1.6 g, Total Carbs: 20.7 g, Protein: 27.5 g.

Easy Fried Cod Filets

This fish comes out light and crispy instead of heavy and greasy which makes it just as healthy as it does delicious. You can use just about any filet of fish for the recipe.

Servings: 4
Prep Time: 10 minutes
Cook Time 15 minutes

3/4 cup milk
2 teaspoons salt
2 to 3 cod filets
3/4 cup plain, fine bread crumbs
1/4 cup grated parmesan cheese
1/4 teaspoon dried leaf thyme
Paprika
Parsley sprigs
Lemon wedges

1. Mix the milk and salt in a shallow bowl.
2. In another bowl mix together the bread crumbs, thyme, and parmesan.
3. Dip each cod filet in the milk mixture then toss it in the bread crumb mix until fully coated.
4. Cook in your air fryer at 360F for 15 minutes, flip the filets halfway through.
5. Sprinkle paprika over the filets while they cool and garnish with parsley and lemon.

Nutrition

Calories: 196, Sodium: 254 mg, Dietary Fiber: 1.2 g, Total Fat: 1.2 g, Total Carbs: 17.4 g, Protein: 23.1 g.

Shrimp & Mango Spring Rolls

These bad boys basically dance all over your taste buds from the tip of the tongue to the back of the throat. There is a little bit of work that goes into these, but they are still fairly simple to create and cook.

Servings: 4
Prep Time: 10 minutes
Cook Time: 10 minutes

- 6 large egg roll wrappers
- 1 large egg
- 12 large shrimp
- Chili pepper to sprinkle
- 12 (3" long) peeled slices of fresh mango
- 24 to 36 small sprigs cilantro

1. Beat the egg in a bowl.
2. Cut each egg roll wrapper in half and brush with beaten egg.
3. Peel each shrimp, leaving the tail on, and place it in the center of the egg roll wrapper as straight as possible.
4. Place mango and a few pieces of cilantro next to each shrimp. Sprinkle lightly with chili pepper.
5. Roll each wrapper around the shrimp and place in the basket.
6. Cook in your air fryer at 400F for 10 minutes, shaking often.

Nutrition

Calories: 776, Sodium: 1370 mg, Dietary Fiber: 6.3 g, Total Fat: 5.3 g, Total Carbs: 150.4 g, Protein: 28.5 g.

Potato Crusted Salmon

Salmon has a rather unique flavor that is not for everyone, but this recipe makes salmon a preferred dish. The crispy potato flakes compliment the taste of salmon without overpowering it completely.

Servings: 4
Prep Time: 10 minutes
Cook Time: 15 minutes

1 lb. salmon fillets (can also use, swordfish or arctic char fillets) 3/4 inch thick
1 egg white
2 tablespoons water
1/3 cup dry instant mashed potatoes
2 teaspoons cornstarch
1 teaspoon paprika
1 teaspoon lemon pepper seasoning

1. Remove skin from the fish and cut it into 4 serving pieces.
2. Mix together the egg white and water.
3. Mix together all of the dry ingredients.
4. Dip the filets into the egg white mixture then press into the potato mix to coat evenly.
5. In your air fryer, cook at 360F for 15 minutes, flip the filets halfway through.

Nutrition

Calories: 176, Sodium: 63 mg, Dietary Fiber: 0.6 g, Total Fat: 7.1 g, Total Carbs: 5.2 g, Protein: 23.4 g.

Fried Fish Tacos

Fish tacos are becoming increasingly popular for many reasons from being excellent street food to making amazing high class restaurant fare. Now you can make fish tacos at home that satisfy the palate of the kids and the sensibilities of mom and dad.

Servings: 8
Prep Time: 5 minutes
Cook Time: 15 minutes

2 lbs. cod
3 cups panko breadcrumbs
3 eggs
2 teaspoons cold water
Salt and pepper, to taste
16 soft tortillas
1 (14 ounce) bag coleslaw mix
2 avocados
1 tomato

1. Beat eggs, water, salt, and pepper together in a bowl.
2. Pour your bread crumbs into a separate bowl.
3. Cut fish into 8 pieces and season with salt and pepper.
4. Dip fish in egg mixture, then roll in panko crumbs to coat evenly.
5. Place them on a pan lined with paper towels to allow the bread crumbs to soak into the fish.
6. Cook in your air fryer at 360F for 15 minutes, flipping halfway through.
7. Serve with tortillas, avocado, coleslaw, and tomatoes.

Nutrition

Calories: 586, Sodium: 567 mg, Dietary Fiber: 8.4 g, Total Fat: 21.5 g, Total Carbs: 62.0 g, Protein: 37.9 g.

Indian Fish Fingers

These work just as well as a main course as they do for a snack. They offer just enough spice and the perfect mixture of soft and crispy that will make you crave this fun and tasty take on fish fingers.

Servings: 4
Prep Time: 35 minutes
Cook Time: 15 minutes

1/2 lb. fish fillet
1 tablespoon finely chopped fresh mint leaves or any fresh herbs
1/3 cup bread crumbs
1 teaspoon ginger garlic paste or ginger and garlic powders
1 hot green chili finely chopped
1/2 teaspoon paprika
Generous pinch of black pepper
Salt, to taste
3/4 tablespoon lemon juice
3/4 teaspoon garam masala powder
1/3 teaspoon rosemary
1 egg

1. Start by removing any skin on the fish, washing, and patting dry.
2. Cut the fish into fingers.
3. In a medium bowl mix together all ingredients except for fish, mint, and bread crumbs.
4. Bury the fingers in the mixture and refrigerate for 30 minutes.
5. Remove the bowl from the fridge and mix in mint leaves.
6. In a separate bowl beat the egg, pour bread crumbs into a third bowl.
7. Dip the fingers in the egg bowl then toss them in the bread crumbs bowl.
8. Cook in air fryer at 360F for 15 minutes, toss the fingers halfway through.

Nutrition

Calories: 187, Sodium: 439 mg, Dietary Fiber: 1.0 g, Total Fat: 8.6 g, Total Carbs: 16.8 g, Protein: 11.0 g.

Old Bay Crab Cakes

Who doesn't love crab cakes? They can be used as an appetizer or a main course and they are bursting with that unmistakable delicious crab flavor. Try these out as crab burgers for something a little different.

Servings: 4
Prep Time: 10 minutes
Cook Time: 20 minutes

2 slices dried bread, crusts removed
Small amount of milk
1 tablespoon mayonnaise
1 tablespoon Worcestershire sauce
1 tablespoon baking powder
1 tablespoon parsley flakes
1 teaspoon Old Bay® Seasoning
1/4 teaspoon salt
1 egg
1 lb. lump crabmeat

1. Crush your bread over a large bowl until it is broken down into small pieces.
2. Add milk and stir until bread crumbs are moistened.
3. Mix in mayo and Worcestershire sauce.
4. Add remaining ingredients and mix well.
5. Shape into 4 patties.
6. Cook in air fryer at 360F for 20 minutes, flip half way through.

Nutrition

Calories: 165, Sodium: 581 mg, Dietary Fiber: 0 g, Total Fat: 4.5 g, Total Carbs: 5.8 g, Protein: 24.7 g.

Salmon Croquettes

Croquette may sound like a fancy word, but it is really just a fried bread combination. That being said, your guests and family will feel pretty fancy eating these tasty little concoctions.

Servings: 4
Prep Time: 10 minutes
Cook Time: 20 minutes

- 1/4 cup organic olive oil mayonnaise
- 4 teaspoons fresh lemon juice
- 2-1/2 teaspoons Dijon mustard
- 1/4 cup finely chopped green onions
- 2 tablespoons minced red bell pepper
- 1/2 teaspoon garlic powder
- 1/4 teaspoon salt
- 1/8 teaspoon ground red pepper
- 2 (6-ounce) packages skinless, boneless pink salmon
- 1 large egg
- 1 cup panko

For serving sauce

- 1 tablespoon olive oil
- 1 tablespoon chopped fresh parsley
- 1 teaspoon finely chopped capers
- 1/2 teaspoon minced garlic
- 1/8 teaspoon salt

1. Combine mayo, lemon juice, mustard, onions, bell pepper, salt, garlic powder, and red pepper.
2. Beat egg and add to mixture.
3. Add salmon and break apart into mixture until it is evenly divided.
4. Mix in panko bread crumbs.
5. Shape mixture into 8 patties and place in basket.
6. Cook in your air fryer at 360F for 20 minutes flipping half way through.
7. Mix together oil, capers, parsley, and salt to serve as a complementary sauce.

Nutrition

Calories: 335, Sodium: 595 mg, Dietary Fiber: 1.9 g, Total Fat: 14.8 g, Total Carbs: 25.1 g, Protein: 25.1 g.

Quick Fried Catfish

Catfish is a southern delicacy that many may have never experienced. This recipe is a great way to experience catfish for either the first time, or just as a new preparation to a favorite meal!

Servings: 4
Prep Time: 5 minutes
Cook Time: 15 minutes

3/4 cup Original Bisquick™ mix
1/2 cup yellow cornmeal
1 tablespoon seafood seasoning
4 catfish fillets (4 to 6 oz each)
1/2 cup ranch dressing
Lemon wedges

1. In a shallow bowl mix together the Bisquick mix, cornmeal, and seafood seasoning.
2. Pat the filets dry, then brush them with ranch dressing.
3. Press the filets into the Bisquick mix on both sides until the filet is evenly coated.
4. Cook in your air fryer at 360F for 15 minutes, flip the filets halfway through.
5. Serve with a lemon garnish.

Nutrition

Calories: 372, Sodium: 532 mg, Dietary Fiber: 1.7 g, Total Fat: 16.1 g, Total Carbs: 27.0 g, Protein: 28.2 g.

Oyster Sandwiches

Oyster sandwiches may not be an every week thing, but they are definitely a nice treat! Not only is this recipe delicious, but it is fairly healthy too, which is a win-win.

Servings: 6
Prep Time: 15 minutes
Cook Time: 20 minutes

Spicy rémoulade sauce

1-1/2 cups mayonnaise
1/4 cup whole-grain mustard
1 garlic clove, minced
1 tablespoon pickle juice
1 tablespoon drained capers
1 teaspoon horseradish
1/4 teaspoon cayenne pepper
1/4 teaspoon hot paprika
1/2 teaspoon hot sauce

Oysters

1 cup buttermilk
Sea salt and freshly ground black pepper
48 oysters, shucked and drained
1 cup all-purpose flour
1/2 cup cornmeal
1/2 cup plain bread crumbs
2 tablespoons Old Bay Seasoning
6 brioche or potato hot dog rolls

1. Combine the mayo, hot sauce, mustard, garlic, pickle juice, capers, paprika, cayenne pepper, and horseradish; mix well.
2. Refrigerate until ready to serve.
3. Mix together the buttermilk, salt, and pepper.
4. Add oysters and let stand.
5. In another bowl, mix together flour, cornstarch, old bay spice, and bread crumbs.
6. Take the oysters out of the buttermilk mix and toss them in the flour mix.
7. Using your air fryer, cook in batches at 360F for 20 minutes, flipping half way through.
8. Serve inside of bun and topped with sauce.

Nutrition

Calories: 615, Sodium: 861.6 mg, Dietary Fiber: 3.8 g, Total Fat: 26.8 g, Total Carbs: 75.2 g, Protein: 18.3 g.

Japanese Style Fried Shrimp

This fried shrimp combines a host of flavors to satisfy the palate. Fast prep and cook times make this recipe perfect for a weeknight family meal. You will love their crisp outside and juicy inside!

Servings: 4
Prep Time: 10 minutes
Cook Time: 10 minutes

- 1 lb. medium shrimp, peeled (tails left on) and deveined
- 1/2 teaspoon salt
- 1/2 teaspoon ground black pepper
- 1/2 teaspoon garlic powder
- 1 cup all-purpose flour
- 1 teaspoon paprika
- 2 eggs
- 1 cup panko crumbs

1. Place your shrimp in a bowl and sprinkle it with the salt, pepper, and garlic powder.
2. In another bowl mix together the flour and the paprika.
3. Beat the eggs into another separate bowl and put the panko crumbs in their own bowl.
4. Dip each shrimp into the flour, then the egg mix, and roll in the panko crumbs until completely covered.
5. Cook at 375F in your air fryer for 10 minutes, shaking a few times.

Nutrition

Calories: 363, Sodium: 777 mg, Dietary Fiber: 2.4 g, Total Fat: 5.4 g, Total Carbs: 44.2 g, Protein: 34.1 g.

Shrimp Wontons

These wontons are awesome because they can be used as an appetizer, side dish, or a main meal. They take a little more work than your average recipe, but the delicious results are worth it.

Servings: 4
Prep Time: 25 minutes
Cook Time: 10 minutes

3/4 lb. shrimp
1 scallion
1/4 teaspoon ginger
Pinch black pepper
1 tablespoon Chinese cooking wine
1 teaspoon soy sauce
Pinch of salt
Wonton wrappers

1. Peel and devein shrimp.
2. Finely chop shrimp and scallions and put them in a mixing bowl.
3. Grate ginger over the shrimp and mix until all ingredients are evenly blended.
4. Mix in wine, soy sauce, salt, and pepper and allow to marinate for 15 minutes.
5. Roll out each of your wonton wrappers.
6. Scoop about 1/2 of shrimp mix in each one, then fold into wonton.
7. Cook in your air fryer at 400F for 10 minutes, shaking often.

Nutrition

Calories: 130, Sodium: 368 mg, Dietary Fiber: 0 g, Total Fat: 1.6 g, Total Carbs: 6.5 g, Protein: 20.3 g.

CHAPTER 9

Vegetables
& Side Dishes

Roasted Corn

Perfectly roasted corn in an air fryer? It sounds impossible, but it's just impossibly good! Enjoy with just about any main dish. Your family will love it.

Servings: 4
Prep Time: 5 minutes
Cook Time: 10 minutes

4 fresh ears of corn
2 teaspoons olive oil
Salt and pepper, to taste

1. Remove the corn husks and wash and pat dry the cob.
2. If you need to, cut down the cob to fit in your basket.
3. Drizzle a little oil over each cob and sprinkle with salt and pepper.
4. Cook at 390°F for 10 minutes using your air fryer, flip halfway through.

Nutrition

Calories: 100, Sodium: 10 mg, Dietary Fiber: 1 g, Fat: 3.3 g, Carbs: 18 g, Protein: 3 g.

Seasoned Potato Wedges

Recipes like this one are what the air fryer was made for. This is the perfect side dish for any meal that goes well with tasty potatoes.

Servings: 4
Prep Time: 10 minutes
Cook Time: 20 minutes

4 russet potatoes
1 tablespoon bacon fat
1 teaspoon paprika
1 teaspoon chili powder
1 teaspoon salt
1/2 teaspoon black pepper

1. Wash potatoes and cut each one into 8 wedges.
2. Warm bacon fat in the microwave for 10 seconds.
3. Combine all of your dry seasoning in a bowl and toss to mix.
4. Add bacon fat to the bowl and stir.
5. Toss the wedges in the bowl and transfer to the basket.
6. Using the air fryer, cook at 390°F for 20 minutes, tossing halfway through.

Nutrition

Calories: 164, Sodium: 604 mg, Dietary Fiber: 5.6 g, Fat: 3.8 g, Carbs: 34.3 g, Protein: 3.8 g.

Home Made
Tater Tots

Tater tots are a fantastic change from French fries and being able to make them from scratch makes a fun and edible activity. Your kids will love them and you will feel better knowing that you made them yourself!

Servings: 3
Prep Time: 40 minutes
Cook Time: 20 minutes

3 russet potatoes
2 tablespoons dehydrated chopped onion
2 tablespoons corn starch
1 tablespoon chives
1 teaspoon garlic powder
1 teaspoon garlic salt

1. Scrub the potatoes and peel them. Mince the chives.
2. Combine 2 tablespoons of hot water and the dehydrated onions in a bowl and set aside.
3. Grate the potatoes into a bowl and fill with cold water. Strain the potatoes and repeat the process to get rid of extra starch.
4. Add corn starch to the potatoes and mix well to combine.
5. Preheat your oven to 400°F.
6. Spread the potatoes out over a baking sheet and bake for 20 minutes.
7. Allow the potatoes to cool, then transfer them to a bowl and mix well with all other ingredients.
8. Scoop out 1 - 2 tablespoons of the mixture and place them in your basket.
9. Using the air fryer, cook at 350°F for 20 minutes. Shake a few times during the cooking process.

Nutrition
Calories: 174, Sodium: 122 mg, Dietary Fiber: 5.2 g, Fat: 0.2 g, Carbs: 40.2 g, Protein: 3.8 g.

Honey Roasted Carrots

Are you looking for something different to go with a chicken or turkey main dish? Check out this mouthwatering side that is a little sweet and a lot of healthy.

Servings: 4
Prep Time: 5 minutes
Cook Time: 12 minutes

3 cups baby carrots
1 tablespoon olive oil
1 tablespoon honey
Salt and pepper, to taste

1. Put the carrots in a bowl, then drizzle over oil and honey.
2. Sprinkle on salt and pepper, then mix well with a wooden spoon.
3. Put the carrots in the basket and cook at 390°F for 12 minutes using your air fryer.
4. For best results, serve immediately.

Nutrition

Calories: 53, Sodium: 17 mg, Dietary Fiber: 0.6 g, Fat: 3.5 g, Carbs: 6.1 g, Protein: 0.2 g.

Onion Rings

Nothing beats a good old fashion onion ring. This recipe puts a little twist on an old favorite, but it still tastes great and is much healthier than traditionally deep-fried onion rings.

Servings: 4
Prep Time: 7 minutes
Cook Time: 7 minutes

1 teaspoon baking powder
1 teaspoon salt
1 cup panko breadcrumbs
2 eggs
1 large Vidalia onion
1 cup all-purpose flour

1. Peel and cut the onion into rings.
2. Combine the flour, salt, and baking powder in a bag and shake well to combine.
3. Add the onions in the bag and toss to coat.
4. Beat the eggs in a shallow bowl.
5. Spread the panko crumbs over a plate.
6. Remove 1 ring at a time, shake off any extra flour, dip in the egg, then dredge through the bread crumb.
7. Add 5 to 7 rings to the air fryer at a time and cook at 390°F for 7 minutes.
8. Flip the rings halfway through and serve hot.

Nutrition

Calories: 186, Sodium: 615 mg, Dietary Fiber: 1.8 g, Fat: 2.6 g, Carbs: 33.3 g, Protein: 7.1 g.

Garlic Parmesan Fries

Fries are always a welcome addition to a meal. But garlic parmesan fries will have your family eating these faster than you can make them. Crispy, cheesy and garlicky, it's a taste combination made in heaven.

Servings: 4
Prep Time: 15 minutes
Cook Time: 30 minutes

2 lbs. russet potatoes
2 tablespoons olive oil
Salt and pepper, to taste
2 tablespoons butter
2 cloves garlic
1/4 cup parmesan
1/4 cup parsley

1. Peel and cut the potatoes into fries.
2. Soak the potatoes in water, drain, and repeat to remove excess starch.
3. Pat the fries dry.
4. Add the fries, oil, salt, and pepper to a bag and shake well.
5. Preheat the fryer to 390°F.
6. Cook the fries in the air fryer for 30 minutes, tossing 2 or 3 times.
7. Towards the end of the cook time, mince the garlic.
8. Heat the butter in a pan and sauté garlic.
9. Remove from heat and add salt, pepper, parmesan, and parsley to the butter stirring well.
10. Combine fries and butter in a bowl and toss to coat before serving.

Nutrition

Calories: 292, Sodium: 142 mg, Dietary Fiber: 5.6 g, Fat: 14.4 g, Carbs: 36.5 g, Protein: 6 g.

Baked Sweet Potato

Sweet potatoes are a fantastic vegetable side that go with just about any main dish. The sweetness easily balances out savory foods. Plus, sweet potatoes are a healthy, vitamin-packed alternative to regular potatoes.

Servings: 3
Prep Time: 5 minutes
Cook Time: 40 minutes

3 sweet potatoes
1 tablespoon olive oil
Salt, to taste

1. Wash sweet potatoes and pat dry.
2. Rub the potatoes with olive oil and sprinkle with salt.
3. Preheat the air fryer to 390°F.
4. Cook in the air fryer for 40 minutes, flipping halfway through.

Nutrition
Calories: 170, Sodium: 45 mg, Dietary Fiber: 4 g, Fat: 4.7 g, Carbs: 33 g, Protein: 2 g.

Roasted Brussels Sprouts

Roasted brussels sprouts in the air fryer turn the vegetable from something your kids won't touch to something that they will beg for.

Servings: 4
Prep Time: 5 minutes
Cook Time: 15 minutes

1 lb. fresh brussels sprouts
5 teaspoons olive oil
1/2 teaspoon kosher salt

1. Toss all of the ingredients together in a bowl.
2. Preheat the air fryer to 390°F.
3. Cook in the air fryer for 15 minutes, shaking 2 - 3 times during the process.

Nutrition

Calories: 99, Sodium: 319 mg, Dietary Fiber: 4.3 g, Fat: 6.2 g, Carbs: 10.3 g, Protein: 3.9 g.

Vermouth
Roasted Mushrooms

Mushrooms usually compliment a main dish, but with this unique recipe, they take center stage.

Servings: 4
Prep Time: 10 minutes
Cook Time: 25 minutes

2 lbs. button mushrooms
1 tablespoon duck fat
1/2 teaspoon garlic powder
2 teaspoons herbs de Provence
2 tablespoons white vermouth

1. Wash the mushrooms and spin dry.
2. Warm up the duck fat, garlic powder, vermouth, and herbs in a skillet for 5 minutes mixing well.
3. Toss the mushrooms in the skillet and transfer to the basket.
4. Using your air fryer, cook at 320°F for 25 minutes. Toss once at the 15-minute mark.

Nutrition
Calories: 92, Sodium: 13 mg, Dietary Fiber: 2.3 g, Fat: 3.8 g, Carbs: 8.1 g, Protein: 7.2 g.

Lemony Green Beans

Green beans have been a staple side since the dawn of cooking. This recipe takes the old favorite and freshens it up with zesty lemon.

Servings: 4
Prep Time: 5 minutes
Cook Time: 12 minutes

1 lb. fresh green beans
1 lemon
Salt and pepper, to taste
1/4 teaspoon olive oil

1. Wash and de-stem the green beans.
2. Put the beans in a bowl and drizzle oil over the top of them.
3. Cut the lemon in half and squeeze fresh lemon juice over the beans.
4. Season with salt and pepper and toss well.
5. Transfer the beans to your basket. Using the air fryer, cook at 390°F for 12 minutes.

Nutrition

Calories: 42, Sodium: 7 mg, Dietary Fiber: 4.3 g, Fat: 0.5 g, Carbs: 9.4 g, Protein: 2.2 g.

Crispy Onion Straws

I love crispy onion straws because they taste great and can be used as a side or a topping on a lot of dishes.

Servings: 4
Prep Time: 30 minutes
Cook Time: 15 minutes

1 large onion
1-2 cups buttermilk
2 cups flour
1 tablespoon paprika
Salt and pepper, to taste
1/2 tablespoon cumin
1/2 tablespoon garlic powder

1. Peel the onion and cut it into the thinnest slices you can.
2. Place the onion in a bowl and cover with buttermilk, allowing it to soak for 20 minutes.
3. Combine the dry ingredients in a shallow bowl.
4. Working one at a time, shake off any extra buttermilk and dredge the onions through the flour mix.
5. Cook using air fryer at 360°F for 8 minutes, shaking often.

Nutrition

Calories: 278, Sodium: 69 mg, Dietary Fiber: 3.3 g, Fat: 1.6 g, Carbs: 56.2 g, Protein: 9.3 g.

Twice Baked Potato

There is a lot of time put into twice baked potatoes, but the end result is worth it and with the air fryer, they come out perfectly crispy on the outside every time.

Servings: 4
Prep Time: 10 minutes
Cook Time: 1 hr 20 minutes

2 russet potatoes
2 teaspoons olive oil
1/4 cup yogurt
1/4 cup milk
2 tablespoons nutritional yeast
1/2 teaspoon salt
1/4 teaspoon pepper
1 cup spinach

1. Scrub the potatoes and allow them to dry.
2. Rub each potato all around with oil.
3. Preheat your air fryer to 390°F.
4. Cook for 30 minutes, turn each potato and cook for another 30 minutes.
5. Let the potatoes cool enough to handle them, then cut them in half vertically.
6. Scoop out the center meat of the potato, leaving enough around the edges to create a "bowl."
7. Transfer the scooped potato to another bowl.
8. Mix the scooped potato, milk, yogurt, yeast, salt, and pepper together to create a smooth filling.
9. Chop the spinach and stir it into the mix.
10. Fill each potato half with the mixture.
11. Lower the temperature on your air fryer to 350°F.
12. Cook each half for an additional 5 minutes.

Nutrition

Calories: 134, Sodium: 324 mg, Dietary Fiber: 4 g, Fat: 3.3 g, Carbs: 21.2 g, Protein: 5.7 g.

Zucchini Fries

If you love the salt and crispness of fries, but don't love the calories, these zucchini fries are a perfect alternative.

Servings: 3
Prep Time: 10 minutes
Cook Time: 20 minutes

3 medium zucchinis
2 eggs
1/2 cup seasoned breadcrumbs
2 tablespoons parmesan cheese
1/4 teaspoon garlic powder
Salt and pepper, to taste

1. Separate the eggs and discard the yolk, setting aside the whites.
2. Peel the zucchinis and cut them into fry-sized sticks.
3. Mix salt and pepper into the egg whites.
4. Mix breadcrumbs, garlic powder, and cheese together in a shallow bowl.
5. Dip the zucchini sticks in the egg, then dredge them through the bread crumb mix.
6. Preheat the air fryer to 320°F and cook for 20 minutes. Toss a few times through the cooking process.

Nutrition

Calories: 105, Sodium: 104 mg, Dietary Fiber: 2.3 g, Fat: 4.3 g, Carbs: 10.6 g, Protein: 8.1 g.

Crispy Roasted Broccoli

Anyone can make a side of broccoli, but you can make this crispy roasted broccoli, which turns the ordinary into extraordinary.

Servings: 2
Prep Time: 45 minutes
Cook Time: 10 minutes

1 lb. broccoli
2 tablespoons plain yogurt
1 tablespoon chickpea flour
1/4 teaspoon turmeric powder
1/2 teaspoon salt
1/2 teaspoon red chili powder

1. Cut broccoli into bite-sized florets and soak in water for 30 minutes.
2. Drain the florets and allow them to dry on a towel.
3. Mix together all the ingredients to create a marinade.
4. Mix the broccoli into the marinade and allow it to sit in the fridge for 15 minutes.
5. Preheat the fryer to 390°F.
6. While the fryer preheats, remove the broccoli from the marinade and shake off any extra.
7. Cook in your air fryer for 10 minutes, tossing halfway through.

Nutrition

Calories: 114, Sodium: 75mg, Dietary Fiber: 7.3 g, Fat: 1.5 g, Carbs: 20.5 g, Protein: 8.5 g.

Fried Chickpeas

As long as you remember to soak your chickpeas the day before, this recipe is not very time intensive. It is awesome because it is healthy, naturally gluten free, and bursting with taste.

Servings: 6
Prep Time: 12 hrs 10 minutes
Cook Time: 15 minutes

2 cups dried chickpeas
1/4 teaspoon salt
3 tablespoons grated parmesan
2 tablespoons chopped cilantro
1 scotch bonnet pepper
2 cloves garlic
Water, to soak the peas

1. Pour the chickpeas in a bowl and cover in water, allow them to absorb water until they double in size, usually overnight.
2. Cook the chickpeas in your air fryer at 360F for about 15 minutes, shaking often.
3. While the chickpeas cook, chop up the pepper, garlic, and cilantro into fine pieces.
4. Mix the vegetable together with the parmesan cheese.
5. Mix the vegetable mix with the chickpeas and serve.

Nutrition

Calories: 271, Sodium: 184 mg, Dietary Fiber: 11.7 g, Total Fat: 5.7 g, Total Carbs: 41.7 g, Protein: 15.5 g.

Skinny Carrot Fries

These skinny fries are a great little snack and a perfect way to get the kids to eat their carrots. They are incredibly simple to make and a delicious reminder that eating vegetables doesn't mean that you need to give up taste.

Servings: 2
Prep Time: 5 minutes
Cook Time: 15 minutes

1 lb. carrots
1 tablespoon corn flour
1 tablespoon olive oil
1 teaspoon finely chopped tarragon
Pinch of salt
Pinch of black pepper

1. Cut carrots into fries.
2. Mix together corn flour and a pinch of pepper in a bowl.
3. Roll fries in corn flour mix, then transfer to a sealable container.
4. Pour in olive oil and toss.
5. Cook at 400F for 15 minutes, tossing frequently.
6. Remove fries and place them back in the sealable container.
7. Sprinkle in tarragon and salt, toss, and serve.

Nutrition
Calories: 167, Sodium: 234 mg, Dietary Fiber: 5.9 g, Total Fat: 7.2 g, Total Carbs: 25.3 g, Protein: 2.2 g.

Crispy Enoki & Onion Fritters

There is so much flavor bursting out of these fritters that it will be hard to have just one. Don't let the long list of ingredients scare you, this recipe is fairly quick and easy to make.

Servings: 4
Prep Time: 10 minutes
Cook Time: 20 minutes

- 2 (3-1/2-ounce) package Enoki mushrooms
- 1 medium onion, finely sliced
- 1/4 cup flour
- 1/4 cup cornstarch
- 1/2 teaspoon baking powder
- 1/2 teaspoon paprika
- Pinch cayenne pepper
- Sea salt
- 1 tablespoon toasted sesame seeds
- 1 large egg
- 2 tablespoons vodka or other liquor
- 1 tablespoon finely sliced chives

1. Cut the tips off of the mushrooms and break them apart into a bowl.
2. Mix onions in with the mushrooms.
3. Combine flour, corn starch, baking powder, paprika, cayenne, 1/2 teaspoon of salt, and sesame seeds, pour into mushroom and onions and mix well.
4. Beat eggs in a separate bowl and mix in vodka.
5. Pour eggs into mushroom mix and work with hands until well mixed.
6. Scoop mix into a muffin tin and bake in your air fryer at 360F for 20 minutes.
7. Sprinkle chives on top and serve.

Nutrition

Calories: 129, Sodium: 23 mg, Dietary Fiber: 1.8 g, Total Fat: 2.7 g, Total Carbs: 18.6 g, Protein: 4.7 g.

Potato Chips

Nothing beats a good crisp potato chip, except for maybe an air fried potato chip with the same great taste, but fewer calories.

Servings: 3
Prep Time: 5 minutes
Cook Time: 30 minutes

3 russet potatoes
1/2 teaspoon olive oil
Sea salt, to taste

1. Scrub potatoes and pat dry.
2. Leave the skin on and cut potatoes into thin slices.
3. Toss the potato slices in oil and sea salt.
4. Preheat your air fryer to 390°F.
5. Cook for 30 minutes, tossing ingredients often.

Nutrition

Calories: 154, Sodium: 13 mg, Dietary Fiber: 5.1 g, Fat: 1 g, Carbs: 33.5 g, Protein: 3.6 g.

California Fried Walnuts

These walnuts are a masterpiece and could be categorized as a snack or dessert. No matter how you look at them they are a nutritious and satisfying snack option that is sure to please almost anyone. Try them sprinkled on salad for a change.

Servings: 16
Prep Time: 10 minutes
Cook Time: 5 minutes

6 cups water
4 cups walnut halves
1/2 cup sugar
1-1/4 teaspoons salt

1. Bring water to boil in a large sauce pan.
2. Add walnuts and boil for 1 minute.
3. Drain and rinse the walnuts, then transfer to a bowl and toss in sugar.
4. Cook at 350F for 5 minutes tossing halfway through.
5. Sprinkle with salt and serve.

Nutrition
Calories: 217, Sodium: 38 mg, Dietary Fiber: 2.1 g, Total Fat: 18.4 g, Total Carbs: 9.3 g, Protein: 7.5 g.

Fried Artichokes

Artichokes have a unique taste that sets off many dishes. This particular recipe brings out their unique flavor with a little zest of lemon and a nice crunch.

Servings: 8
Prep Time: 15 minutes
Cook Time: 10 minutes

2 tablespoons fine sea salt
1 teaspoon ground black pepper
Juice and rind of 2 lemons
8 American globe artichokes

1. Fill a medium mixing bowl with water and add lemon juice and rinds and set aside.
2. Using a paring knife cut off as much of the hard outer shell that you can and trim the stem down to about 2 inches.
3. Immediately place the artichokes in the lemon water to prevent the artichokes from browning.
4. Dry artichokes with a paper towel and sprinkle with salt and pepper.
5. Cook in your air fryer at 350F for 10 minutes shaking often.
6. Remove artichokes from basket and place them on their heads.
7. Spoon out the choke and serve.

Nutrition

Calories: 81, Sodium: 1557 mg, Dietary Fiber: 9.2 g, Total Fat: 0.3 g, Total Carbs: 18.6 g, Protein: 5.5 g.

Fried Plantains

This recipe for fried plantains is relatively healthy, but your taste buds will never know that this dish isn't as decadent as it tastes. Delicious as a side to all kinds of chicken dishes, beans or even grilled veggies.

Servings: 3
Prep Time: 1 hour 5 minutes
Cook Time: 10 minutes

2 ripe plantains
1 cup panko bread crumbs
1/2 cup orange juice

1. Peel plantains and cut them into 1/4 inch thick circles.
2. Pour orange juice into a bowl and soak plantain slices in the orange juice for at least an hour in the fridge.
3. Toss slices in panko until covered evenly and place in basket.
4. Cook at 320F for 10 minutes, tossing a few times.

Nutrition

Calories: 306, Sodium: 269 mg, Dietary Fiber: 4.4 g, Total Fat: 2.4 g, Total Carbs: 68.3 g, Protein: 6.6 g.

Rosemary
Sweet Potato Fries

Sweet potatoes and fresh rosemary are a match made in heaven and a perfect side item for mains containing chicken or lamb. This recipe is bursting with flavor, and though the prep time is long, it is easy to perfect this dish.

Servings: 2
Prep Time: 1 hr 10 minutes
Cook Time: 20 minutes

2 medium sweet potatoes
1-2 tablespoons coconut oil
1 tablespoon fresh rosemary
Sea salt and pepper

1. Cut sweet potatoes into fries.
2. Soak the fries in a bowl of water for an hour.
3. Remove fries and pat dry with paper towels.
4. Put the fries in a dry bowl and add coconut oil, rosemary, salt, and pepper, and toss.
5. Cook at 400F for 20 minutes, shaking often.

Nutrition
Calories: 197, Sodium: 478 mg, Dietary Fiber: 4.3 g, Total Fat: 10.6 g, Total Carbs: 24.7 g, Protein: 2.6 g.

CHAPTER 10

Desserts

Mini Chocolate Molten Lava Cakes

The name says it all, but these little lava cakes are simply wonderful and easier to make than it sounds! Enjoy the warm, gooey chocolate inside.

Servings: 4
Prep Time: 10 minutes
Cook Time: 10 minutes

4 ramekins
1-1/2 tablespoons self-rising flour
3-1/2 tablespoons baker's sugar
1/3 cup unsalted butter
1/3 cup dark chocolate pieces
2 eggs
Cooking spray

1. Spray the ramekins and set them aside.
2. Melt the chocolate and butter in a bowl, in the microwave, for 30 seconds at a time, mixing after each time.
3. Beat the eggs and mix in the sugar. Stir egg and chocolate mixtures together, then add flour and mix well.
4. Preheat your air fryer to 375°F.
5. Fill each ramekin with the batter about 3/4 of the way.
6. Bake in your fryer for 10 minutes, then serve warm.

Nutrition

Calories: 370, Sodium: 234 mg, Dietary Fiber: 2.1 g, Fat: 31.3 g, Carbs: 17.6 g, Protein: 4.3 g.

Fried Banana S'mores

This recipe is so good and so easy, it is almost criminal not to try it at least once.

Servings: 4
Prep Time: 5 minutes
Cook Time: 7 minutes

- 4 bananas
- 3 tablespoons mini semi-sweet chocolate chips
- 3 tablespoons mini peanut butter chips
- 3 tablespoons mini marshmallows
- 3 tablespoons graham cracker cereal

1. Preheat the air fryer to 390°F.
2. Cut the bananas lengthwise on the inside of the curve, being careful not to cut all the way through.
3. Fill the inside of the banana with chocolate chips, peanut butter chips, and marshmallows.
4. Press graham cracker pieces into any open areas.
5. Put the bananas in the fryer, leaning on each other to keep them upright.
6. Cook for 7 minutes and let cool slightly before serving.

Nutrition

Calories: 159, Sodium: 14 mg, Dietary Fiber: 3.3 g, Fat: 1.6 g, Carbs: 37.3 g, Protein: 2.3 g.

Monkey Bread

Monkey bread is a dessert staple mostly because it takes few ingredients and is really easy to make. It's also yummy!

Servings: 4
Prep Time: 7 minutes
Cook Time: 7 minutes

1 cup self-rising flour
1 cup non-fat Greek yogurt
1 teaspoon sugar
1/2 teaspoon cinnamon

1. Mix the flour and yogurt until it forms a dough. Roll the dough into a circle, then cut it into fourths.
2. Flatten each quarter and cut it into 8 pieces, then roll them into balls.
3. Combine cinnamon and sugar into a bag and shake well to mix.
4. Add 8 balls to the bag and shake to cover.
5. Preheat the air fryer to 375°F.
6. Put the balls in a loaf pan that fits your basket.
7. Cook in your fryer for 7 minutes.

Nutrition

Calories: 156, Sodium: 17 mg, Dietary Fiber: 1 g, Fat: 0.3 g, Carbs: 30.1 g, Protein: 7.2 g.

Blueberry Apple Crumble

This dessert is so good you wouldn't know it was healthy! You can try substituting different fruits to change out the seasonal fruit flavors.

Servings: 2
Prep Time: 10 minutes
Cook Time: 15 minutes

2 ramekins
1 red apple
1/2 cup blueberries
1/4 cup plus 1 tablespoon flour
2 tablespoons sugar
1/2 teaspoon ground cinnamon
2 tablespoons butter

1. Finely dice the red apples.
2. Mix the fruit in one bowl and all other ingredients in another.
3. Preheat the air fryer to 350°F.
4. Put the fruit in ramekins and sprinkle the flour mixture over it.
5. Bake in the fryer for 15 minutes.

Nutrition

Calories: 367, Sodium: 206 mg, Dietary Fiber: 5.8 g, Fat: 16.4 g, Carbs: 54.2 g, Protein: 2.2 g.

Apple Pie to Go

This handheld dessert is great for a family picnic or after school treat.

Servings: 10
Prep Time: 20 minutes
Cook Time: 8 minutes

3 red apples
1 tablespoon lemon juice
2 teaspoons flour
2 teaspoons cinnamon
2 teaspoons brown sugar
1/2 teaspoon nutmeg
1/2 teaspoon ground cloves
10 sheets of filo pastry
3/4 cups butter

1. Set the pastry out to thaw, then slice and chop the apples. Mix all of your ingredients, except for butter to create apple pie filling.
2. Unroll the filo and cover them with a damp towel. Melt the butter in the microwave for about 40 seconds.
3. Place 1 filo on a piece of parchment paper and brush with butter. Scoop 1/3 cup of the filling into the center of your filo.
4. Fold up the bottom of the filo sheet on top of the bottom of the apple pie filling.
5. Next, fold 1/3 of the length of the pastry over the filling. Then, continue to fold the filling up like you are folding a flag, stopping once or twice to brush the pastry with butter.
6. When it's completely folded, give it one more brush of butter all around.
7. Repeat these steps and cook 2 or 3 at a time using the air fryer at 320°F for 8 minutes, flipping halfway through.

Nutrition

Calories: 211, Sodium: 166 mg, Dietary Fiber: 1.9 g, Fat: 14.4 g, Carbs: 20.5 g, Protein: 1.6 g.

Chocolate Chip Muffins

These muffins could pull double duty as breakfast, but they are so rich that they really deserve to be considered a dessert.

Servings: 6
Prep Time: 10 minutes
Cook Time: 15 minutes

1/2 cup self-rising flour
1 tablespoon cocoa powder
1/4 teaspoon baking soda
1/4 cup sugar
1 tablespoon honey
2 tablespoons plain yogurt
4 tablespoons milk
2 tablespoons coconut oil
1/2 teaspoon vanilla extract
1 teaspoon apple cider vinegar
2 tablespoons chocolate chips

1. Mix the flour and cocoa powder.
2. Add baking soda and sugar to the flour and mix well.
3. In a separate bowl mix yogurt, milk, oil, and vanilla.
4. Create a well in the center of the flour mix and pour in the yogurt mix.
5. Add the vinegar and stir until ingredients are mixed. The batter does not need to be smooth.
6. Mix in the chocolate chips. Pour the batter into cupcake liners.
7. Preheat the air fryer to 320°F.
8. Cook muffins for 15 minutes until golden brown.

Nutrition

Calories: 149, Sodium: 64 mg, Dietary Fiber: 0.7 g, Fat: 6.1 g, Carbs: 22.6 g, Protein: 2.1 g.

Blackberry Hand Pies

These pies are so delicious, you won't be able to get enough of them. They remind me of the Little Debbie pies I used to eat as a kid.

Servings: 6
Prep Time: 30 minutes
Cook Time: 10 minutes

1 package refrigerated pie dough
1 egg
12 ounces fresh blackberries
1/4 cup sugar
3 tablespoons all-purpose flour
2 tablespoons lemon juice
1/2 teaspoon cinnamon

1. Cut the blackberries in half and put them in a saucepan. Mix in the flour, sugar, lemon juice, and cinnamon.
2. Cook the mixture on medium heat, mashing the blackberries with a wooden spoon as you go.
3. Turn off the heat and set the mixture aside. Roll out your pie crust until it is about 1/4 inch thick.
4. Cut 6 equal circles out of the pie crust. Spoon equal amounts of the filling into the center of each circle.
5. Beat the egg in a bowl.
6. Wet the outside of each circle with egg, then fold the crust in half over the filling.
7. Press down the edges all around the outside to seal.
8. Preheat your air fryer to 380°F. Brush the tops of each pie with egg.
9. Cook 2 at a time in the fryer for 10 minutes.

Nutrition

Nutritional Info: Calories: 124, Sodium: 69 mg, Dietary Fiber: 3.2 g, Fat: 3.9 g, Carbs: 21.1 g, Protein: 2.2 g.

Buttermilk
Banana Blueberry Bread

There is no way that you can go wrong with this dessert bread that leans toward the healthy side but is still bursting with flavor.

Servings: 12
Prep Time: 15 minutes
Cook Time: 25 minutes

1-3/4 cups all-purpose flour
1 teaspoon baking powder
1/8 teaspoon baking soda
1/4 teaspoon salt
1/2 cup unsalted butter
1 cup sugar
2 eggs
1/4 cup buttermilk
1/2 teaspoon vanilla extract
3 ripe bananas
1 cup blueberries

1. You will need 3 or 4 bread pans small enough to fit in your fryer. Mix flour, baking soda, baking powder, and salt in a bowl.
2. Beat together butter and sugar until creamed. Beat in eggs, buttermilk, and vanilla.
3. Add bananas and mix in until the mixture is well combined. Continue to mix while slowly adding the flour mixture.
4. Add the blueberries and mix a few more times until incorporated.
5. Grease your pans and pour an even amount of batter into each one.
6. Place the pan on your wire rack. Using your air fryer, cook at 320°F for 25 minutes.

Nutrition

Nutritional Info: Calories: 243, Sodium: 135 mg, Dietary Fiber: 1.6 g, Fat: 8.8 g, Carbs: 39.6 g, Protein: 3.5 g.

KITCHEN UNIT CONVERSION

1 teaspoon	= 1/3 tbsp	= 4.9 ml
1 dessertspoon	= 2 tsp	= 9.9 ml
1 tablespoon	= 1.5 dstsp / 3 tsp	= 14.8 ml
1 fuid ounce	= 2 tbsp / 6 tsp	= 29.6 ml
1 cup	= 16 tbsp / 48 tsp	= 236.6 ml
1 quart	= 4 cup	= 946 ml
1 gal	= 4 quart / 16 cup	= 3.79 l
1 ounce	= 2 tbsp	= 28.4 g
1 pounds	= 16 oz	= 453.6 g

www.ingramcontent.com/pod-product-compliance
Lightning Source LLC
Chambersburg PA
CBHW051804100526
44592CB00016B/2551